AF343506

My Great Education
Student. 19-Years Old.
Bread-and-Butter Work: Prostitute

Laura D.

MY GREAT EDUCATION
Student. 19-Years Old.
Bread-and-Butter Work: Prostitute

With the collaboration of Marion Kirat

Max Milo
TÉMOIGNAGE

Max Milo Éditions, Paris, 2023
www.maxmilo.com
ISBN : 978-2-31501-226-8

To my sister in the shadows…

"One word placed on this sheet, and it all begins... The fusion between paper and ink, between you and me... Love, one transcending the other, the other responding to it. The moment when the two become 'one'; writing, our adventure, this book. This moment that thrills me. The reality of words, of facts, the horror put into writing... The horror of a student time quotient... A book, talking about Laura, but Laura is more than one person... She is too many people at once, we have to open our eyes, and react..."

This book was written in collaboration with Marion Kirat, a 23-year-old translation student.

Introduction

Don't Close Your Eyes

He's now standing in front of me, his boxers at his feet. In my underwear, I watch him stare at me for a long time. I know that in less than a minute, he'll ask me to sit down next to him, and after that, my body won't belong to me for an hour. An hour at 100 euros.

My name is Laura, I'm 19 years old. I'm a modern languages student and I'm forced to prostitute myself to pay for my studies.

I'm not alone. It seems that 40,000 other students are doing the same. Everything followed a strange logic, without me really realizing that I was falling.

I wasn't born with a silver spoon in my mouth. I've never known luxury or ease, but until this year, I've never lacked for anything. My thirst for learning and my convictions always made me think that my student years would be the most beautiful, the most carefree. I never thought that my first year at university would turn into a nightmare that would send me running away from my hometown.

At 19, you don't prostitute yourself for pocket money. You don't sell your body to buy clothes or buy coffee. You do it when you're in need, convincing yourself that it's only temporary, just long enough to pay your bills, rent and food. Student prostitutes are not the kind you'd find on the street. They're not drug addicts, they're not undocumented, and they don't all come from poor backgrounds. They may be white-skinned, French and from families of modest means. What they all have in common is a desire to study in a country where education is increasingly expensive. The story you are about to read takes place in a large French city. I've called it V. to protect my parents. They mustn't know. They must never know. I'm their almost model daughter. Stubborn but not slovenly.

Of course, I can be criticized for not keeping a crummy job to get out of the doldrums. Most student prostitutes, as was my case, have a little job on the side but still can't get out of the red. Prostitution and its astronomical rates are far too great a temptation when you're short of money and need to find it in a hurry.

This is my story, and although it wasn't easy to tell it, my primary motivation was to lift the veil on the hypocrisy surrounding student prostitution. The precarious living conditions of students today can no longer be ignored. For the time being, too few people are aware of the existence of this scourge.

The aim of this testimony is to raise awareness and change things, so that destitute female students never again need to sell their bodies to pay for their studies. So that we are no longer just shocked by trafficking in other countries, but also focus our efforts on French cases.

And so that we don't let this happen again, so that we don't turn a blind eye.

Chapter 1

The Invitation

September 4, 2006

I'm walking at a leisurely pace on the university campus of V. Today is no ordinary day, as I'm enrolling in LEA, Spanish and Italian.

Two weeks ago, I received a letter telling me that I had to go to the university secretary's office at 2.30 p.m. to submit my application and obtain my student card. I was overwhelmed with excitement and rushed to gather all the necessary documents. There's a lot of paperwork, but I got through it. The most exhilarating part was integrating the baccalauréat transcript, as it marks the end of an era in a very concrete way. I also went to take some photos in a hurry in the metro, where I'm wearing a broad smile, a winning smile.

When I got up this morning, I carefully studied the metro route to get to the university on time. I didn't want to miss the registration. I even cheated on public transport because I didn't have enough money to pay for my ticket. I promised myself I wouldn't do it again this year, and that I'd buy a season ticket, even if it was expensive. I'm convinced that university will change a lot of things in my life.

On the metro, I couldn't stand still, overexcited at the prospect of discovering the place where I was going to study and spend so much time. My walkman, to which I'm usually hooked, hadn't been able to quell my exacerbated enthusiasm. I even checked three times to make sure I had all the paperwork to register. I couldn't imagine finding myself there and being told, "Sorry, Miss, but your file is incomplete, so you can't receive your card. You'll have to come back. No, I was becoming a student today, not some other day.

I was so nervous that I almost missed my stop. At the last moment, the cheerful voices of a group of young people snapped me out of my reverie. They were jostling to get off the train, which reminded me that I was getting off there too. I'm going to have to come to terms with my new status: I'm a student now, not a high school student. I'm 18 and a half.

I arrived on campus at 2 p.m. sharp. I didn't really know where to go when I left the metro, so I followed the group of students. Realizing that I still had some time to spare, I wandered around a bit to get a feel for the place. I look at a map posted outside the metro station to see exactly where I am, so as not to get lost. The campus looks like a real village. There are even signs to indicate the various buildings. On the map, I spot what will be my future place of study: "Faculté de langues, bâtiment F." Building F, that's where I'll be studying this year. At this very moment, I can't wait to get to know it, to go up and down its steps like a regular, to know which shortcut to take to reach it. I can't wait to be part of this world.

I decide to take a quick look before signing up. I can't possibly go home without seeing where I'll be studying for my bachelor's degree for the next three years. Once outside, I squint against the September sun, reminiscent of last summer. The building is rather plain, but I don't care. In my eyes today, it's synonymous with the future.

I chose modern languages a little out of spite, I admit. I wanted to go into marketing, and join a school that would offer me outstanding training. I've always been a dynamic person who likes responsibility. I like being constantly stimulated and the challenge that a sale can present. I think I also wanted to have a very clear vision of the world of work as quickly as possible. I wanted to be prepared as best I could for my future job. I was looking for a complete break with the high school environment, which had been a burden for me, with its protectionism and childishness. And, let's be honest, after business school, finding a job is often much easier than after university. And a well-paying one at that.

But this dream is impossible for me at the moment. Schools are far too expensive for me. And taking out a loan requires a multi-year commitment, something I can't afford. Basically, I don't even think my application would have been accepted. Beyond the total repayment, I can't even make regular monthly payments at the moment. So I've given up on that track and am now strategically studying modern languages. I'm convinced that after my LEA degree in Spanish and Italian, I'll be able to switch to a business school, where a command of modern languages is essential. What's more, Latin America has taken off economically in recent years, and with my Spanish and Italian, I'll be ready to attack. And who knows, maybe I'll overtake everyone else with this extra cultural baggage? In front of the F-building, I'm full of dreams.

I'm not to be pitied, I've always had clothes on my back and food on my plate. But I don't know the ease and carefreeness of money. My father works as a laborer and my mother is a nurse. Both earn just minimum wage, with two children to raise. Just enough to make ends meet, but never a surplus. I don't qualify for any grants, because I'm one of those countless students who find themselves in the fatal bracket: a long way from what could be called rich, but not poor enough to receive student aid. After adding up the two family incomes, the government decides that my parents can support me. There's no way out: I have to make do with what we don't have.

I cut my walk short, because I really want to get to the secretariat on time. I can't hold on any longer, I want to have my student card in my hands. I'm almost running.

Once there, I'm faced with a line of people going right up to the outside of the building. I patiently wait, novice that I am. They did say 2.30 p.m. *imperatively*. This is my first taste of student life, which often consists of waiting for hours in front of administrative counters.

Just as I'm heading towards the queue, two girls wearing different-colored T-shirts literally throw themselves at me.

- Hi, are you in your first year?
- Yes, and you?" I said with a rather surprised smile.

One of the girls looks at me strangely. It's not the answer she's expecting and, apparently, she has no intention of getting into a conversation with me. Soon, however, she smiles back: I'm easy prey.

Their only reason for approaching me is to get me to sign up for student social security. I quickly understand from their discourse that they are doing this job before classes resume, and are paid on commission. They're obviously in competition, or even at war, because without making any violent gestures, they're constantly interrupting each other's conversations, almost jostling each other to get in my face. I don't really understand what I'm supposed to do, as all this is new to me. They speak fast and badly, and I only catch every other word. They're both trying to make the most convincing pitch, and their speech is becoming totally incomprehensible. I simply revel in this surreal spectacle, while feeling sorry for them. They're doing this to earn a bit of money, and I'll bet that in life, they're as gentle as lambs.

\- So, have you made a choice?

The two wrestlers look at me, the fight's over. They appeal to my judgment to decide. I didn't listen.

\- Uh… it's just that… I've already got Social Security!

Yes, of course, that's a good excuse. One of them, obviously disappointed and considering she has no more time to waste with me, leaves immediately. The other one lets me go after a few minutes, trying however one last time to make me believe that sometimes, two social protections are better than one and that mine might not be the best, *so if you'd reconsider your choice for a moment, you'd realize that…* blah.

Faced with such a meaningless plea, I step aside to join the queue. It's 2.30 p.m., time for my appointment, but it's certainly not done to walk past everyone, even with very good explanations, to get into the secretariat. So I decide to wait quietly and take a seat behind a huge guy. I look at his summons, the same as mine. It says "2 p.m." in red marker right in the middle of the sheet. 14 hours! But how long has he been there?

Off to the side, I can hear the voices of the regulars, the "old-timers" in their fourth or fifth year, grumbling about the immobility of the queue. It must be the same thing every year. But never mind, I don't have the energy or inclination to get angry today. So I'm not throwing a tantrum, or joining in the general protest.

After half an hour, I begin to wonder if I've been forgotten. I intercept a man wearing a university badge.

- I'm sorry, but I had an appointment at 2:30. I've been waiting for half an hour.

As I speak, I wave my summons in his face. Without even glancing at it, he scornfully replies:

- Yes, mademoiselle, like everyone else here.

- So? I keep waiting? Am I really going to pass today?

- We do what we can.

"We do what we can…" That's not an answer! I've just had my first confrontation with the university administration and it's not exactly a victory, nor a relief.

Faced with such an evasive answer, I decide to wait some more. Inwardly, I reproach myself for not having brought a book with me; I would have passed the time intelligently.

I rummage in my bag anyway, but nothing, not even a newspaper, or a stupid leaflet to read. I regret having sent the two girls packing so quickly; I could at least have taken a brochure from them, that would have kept me busy for five minutes.

Stupidly, I dressed up today. I wore very old heels, as if I were going to an important meeting. But now, standing in line, I hate myself for making such a choice. If I dared, I'd go barefoot.

After an hour and a half's wait, I finally reach the secretariat. I look around at all the busy desks to see who can free up a seat for me first. I'm mumbling words, tired from the day. My good mood is gone, I just want to get my card and go.

At last, a young woman beckons. I rush over to her with a smile on my face, happy to know that I'll soon be finished. She looks at me as if I've just made some lame joke that only makes me laugh. She's not exactly the kind of girl who'd like to get her pep going again!

Then comes the tricky part of the bill.

- Paying by cheque?

Yes, my mother wrote me the check last week. A blank cheque. I can still hear her saying to me: "Laura, be careful not to lose it! Just imagine if someone were to find it!" I've always had a notion of money, and as soon as that check was in my hand, I realized the power it possessed. I carefully stored it in a pouch, which I then placed in my locked desk drawer. I'm the only one who can open it, and although I trust my boyfriend, with whom I live, I prefer to take precautions. You never know.

- Yes, by cheque!

- So, as you don't have a grant, but you do have student social security, that gives us a total of… 404 euros 60!

What a ridiculous total! I hand her the check, trying to hide my grimace. Without a word, she stamps, scribbles signs all over my papers and points me to the student card counter. The whole thing is folded in two minutes.

The man in charge of the cards is no friendlier, almost snatching my school certificate out of my hand. In one mechanically regulated gesture, he prints my student card on plastic, hands it to me and tears off the next sheet.

I don't care anymore, I finally have my student card. This is it, a new page in my life is opening! I'm confident, serene, I hold my future in my hands, on this stupid piece of plastic.

Laura D. 1st year LEA Spanish.

Classy.

I walk back to the metro, feeling calm.

Chapter 2

The Requirement

September 8, 2006

I cross the threshold of my apartment, where I live with my boyfriend Manu, after a day's work at the restaurant. We've been dating for a year and moved in together two months ago.

It was a time when I was desperately looking for a solution for my accommodation at the beginning of the year. I didn't have a penny, and my parents couldn't help me financially. What's more, they don't live in V. As for me, I'd known since my baccalaureate results that I'd have to study there. Manu had already been living there since the start of his physics studies, and I was looking forward to joining him in the city. So I started looking for an apartment. I scoured the Crous and its classified ads to find a maid's room. I soon realized that a real apartment was far too expensive, if not totally unaffordable. All I wanted was a roof over my head, but even that seemed out of reach. I didn't expect anything luxurious. My finances wouldn't allow it anyway.

I was at a dead end. As I wasn't on a scholarship, I didn't get any state aid and my parents couldn't afford to pay 200 euros a month in rent. I didn't get any housing benefit either. Apart from finding a job or giving up my studies, I couldn't see any way out. The Crous favored students with grants for housing in student rooms. A lot of students work on the side, but it's often the same students who fail their exams or give up their studies mid-year. I couldn't put an end to my studies, I knew that my future was at stake. Giving up my studies for a job meant putting an end to my ambitions.

I continued to search frantically for a miracle in the pages of the free newspapers where there were ads. At the same time, I even went to foster homes to ask around. I tried to convince myself that this was the only chance I had left to study, and that once there, I could try to find something else. But the idea of staying in a hostel at night made me shudder, the situation seemed so demeaning.

I was desperate to find a satisfactory solution. One day, when I was crying with rage, Manu jumped at the chance.

- We can live together! That would be great! Between the two of us, we'd be able to find a rent that wasn't too expensive and we'd be together all the time!

Her eyes sparkled. I liked the idea, but my financial difficulties were holding me back.

- Manu, I can't, I've got no money! I barely have enough for a maid's room, so an apartment for two?

- You'll be able to find a job alongside your studies, and college won't take up that much of your time!

I had my reservations. Manu comes from a relatively well-off family and sometimes doesn't realize all the expenses I have to face. To convince me that I could manage to combine my studies with paid work, Manu showed me the university website where the course timetable was posted. I had a lot, but it was manageable. I was seduced by this little piece of the dream that Manu was offering me.

- You see, you can do it, that's for sure! Say yes, it'll be great to be together all the time! And when it comes down to it, you've got no choice!

It's true that I didn't really have a choice. I jumped for joy into his arms. The very next day, Manu welcomed me into his apartment. For me, it was the ultimate luxury. An apartment with its own bedroom in the center of V., I felt like a princess in this palace! I set down my two heavy suitcases in the hallway and started twirling around the apartment, dragging her along with me.

My parents were relieved by this solution, even if they didn't like Manu very much. They preferred it to knowing their daughter was doing a lousy job, or worse, sleeping rough.

I worked all summer in a restaurant down the road, so I could at least pay for the groceries. The little I had left over would give me a little pocket money.

That's our deal: he pays the rent and the bills, and I take care of the rest, given my financial situation. In fact, although he doesn't tell me, I know for a fact that he doesn't pay the rent. His mother pays him every month, plus a generous allowance. I don't say anything about it, I love him too much and, living with him, I consider it normal to contribute to the expenses within my means. I manage as best I can. Sometimes, when I go home to my parents, I take what I find in the fridge or what my mother gives me. This summer, it all worked out perfectly. We were happy as we were, concocting little meals together and sometimes going out with friends for a drink. Most of the time, we stayed in front of the TV, me snuggled up in his arms, him always with a joint in his mouth. With my boyfriend by my side, everything seemed so much easier.

Tonight, I come home exhausted from work, after two hours of overtime which I know I won't be paid for. I'm being totally exploited by this job, but it's the only solution I've found for the time being to make a financial contribution. I also know that with this job, like this all year round, I'd be tired all the time, but for the moment, I can't really do any better. I'll find something else when I've got my timetable, when I know exactly what time I have class.

Manu is there, in front of the TV. I give him a lively "hello" as I sit down next to him and plant a huge kiss on his mouth. Something strange happens: he doesn't respond to my enthusiasm.

- What's going on? Is everything okay?

- Yes, I'm fine," he replies evasively.

- Are you sure about this? It really doesn't look…

Manu turns off the TV and finally looks at me. He hesitates for a moment, then suddenly decides:

- Laura, we're moving in together this year and I want you to contribute to the rent.

I pause, still staring at him.

- Yes, I understand. But I don't earn much at the restaurant. How much do you want me to give you?

- Half the rent, 300 euros. You see, I'm not going to be able to manage on my own…

All alone! What a liar! He knows full well that I barely earn that kind of money from my waitressing job, and that once I'd paid him, I'd have nothing left. To cheer myself up, I tell myself that this is my chance to stop waitressing and find another job.

- All right, I'll have to find another job, I guess.

- Yes, I think you're right. Then for the shopping, we'll take it in turns every two weeks, how's that?

He's also asking me to do all the shopping? I can't believe it!

Lack of money always puts people in such an embarrassing position that they don't dare reply. I simply nod:

- Okay, suit yourself.

I sit down on the sofa and turn on the TV, so I don't have to talk. It's the only way I've found to cut short the awkward silence that has built up between us. In the evenings, I fall asleep in his arms, trying to convince myself that these money issues are normal and won't separate us.

Two days later, I signed up with a telemarketing company for a part-time job.

Chapter 3

Back to School

September 17, 2006

With my timetable in hand, I run to make sure I don't miss my first class. I've just come out of the secretary's office, where I've just done my pedagogical registration. I thought I'd been relieved of all administrative obligations after the interminable wait the other day, but I was wrong!

After administrative registration, I had to go to the modern languages building to register for classes. I only have around twenty hours of classes spread over the week. I was looking forward to this timetable so that I could organize and structure my life. I'll be able to continue working alongside my studies. Starting tomorrow, I'll be able to call the telemarketing company to review my working hours.

The whole procedure was rather quick, and I was quickly given my timetable, but I'm now late for my first class. A glance at the paper tells me that I have to go to the third floor for a Spanish civilization class. I run up the stairs, eager to learn.

I enter the room slowly, the other students are already seated. I mumble an inaudible "excuse me". The professor gives me a fleeting glance, then returns to his roll-call list.

- You are?

- Laura, Laura D.

After scribbling something on his paper, he beckons me to sit down. I take a seat next to another girl. The female sex is overwhelmingly in the majority in the room, and certainly in the whole class.

The teacher asks us to fill in a form to get to know each other better. Ah, the famous cards! So far, not really any different from high school, they were bound to ask us for one for each class. By the end of the week, I'll probably end up answering them in just a few seconds.

The form includes a "Career plans" box. I think long and hard about this question. Do I know what I really want to do? I want to be in business, yes, but in what exactly? I have a lot of convictions about the responsibilities that would suit me perfectly, but is there a given denomination, a precise job for that? I write down everything I dream of, I entrust all my expectations to this unknown person, all the hopes that university represents for me. Something is missing.

I chew my pencil and look up at the ceiling. Then, after a few minutes, I write at the very bottom of my inventory of dreams for the future:

Live life to the full.

It's not, of course, the answer the teacher expects, if he expects one in particular, but it's the one that fits me best.

We begin the course, and with each passing minute I thank the heavens for giving me the gift of being in this room. My mother had to pay over 400 euros for me to be here, but she did it without hesitation, knowing full well that my future depended on it, she who has always wanted only the best for her daughters. I'm going to learn, I'm going to succeed.

The course is in Spanish only. My father is Spanish, and although he never spoke to me in his mother tongue, I learned Spanish during our vacations with his family.

The teacher passes us a sheet with the list of books for this year.

- If you want to succeed, you'll have to read them all very carefully, taking lots of notes.

I drink in his words. Yes, of course I'll read them all, I've always loved reading, it's no problem!

- There are some you won't find in the library. I've been asking for them, but they haven't arrived yet, so you'll probably have to pay for them out of your own pocket, agree to lend them to you...

I'm much less happy about that. Books in their original language are always very expensive, at least 15 euros, and while I hope to be able to afford one or two, I can't afford all these extra costs.

I look at the card, fearing its completeness. I grit my teeth as I discover a dozen books to buy. I quickly put it away in my bag, I don't want to spoil my day. I've got plenty of time to think about it.

- Furthermore, I do not accept repeated unjustified absences. After three absences, I will not allow you to take the exam in my subject.

It's clear and precise. It's up to me whether I really want to succeed or not. The cards are in my hands.

The hour passed quickly, and I wasn't bored for a single second, unlike in high school when I looked at my watch every five minutes. I make my way to the next class, where I discover a real amphitheater for the first time. I'm so impressed I can't even breathe. I'm not the only one; many people stop for a few seconds to admire the immense hall. Only the repeaters hurry to choose a seat. For them, it's the same as for enrolments: they know what's going on, they can afford to be blasé.

I contemplate the place, already knowing that I'm going to love learning here. I'll be a needle in a haystack, unnoticed and unknown. Professors won't interrupt their classes to give me a reflection on my latest assignment. University is a service: we're offered a course, which we're free to attend or not, which we're free to take as we see fit. I'm just one number among many, but now I have to choose whether to take it or not. I like this atmosphere where we're already considered adults.

I've finally got it, my real break with high school. Even after just one day here, I can feel that everything is going to be different. My senior year left indelible marks on me, suffering I'm sure I won't have to face here.

In my final year of high school, I remember a history teacher publicly humiliating me in front of the whole class by attacking me personally. After a surprise test in which I had just received a very mediocre mark, he called me "incapable", to which I responded with a most indifferent flutter of my eyelashes. I was perfectly able to take his comments about my little person in stride, but in reality it didn't make any difference to me, because this teacher didn't interest me in the least and always treated me like a child. The drama came with the next sentence.

- No reaction, Laura? I'm not congratulating you, but it seems to me that you should seriously reconsider your future, which is shaky at the moment.

All this cruelty for my first and only below-average grade! But he didn't stop there.

- Admit it, you're very dissipated, and you're not taking your lessons properly. What goes around comes around, Laura. Your parents seem very irresponsible to me…

Hearing the word "parents" made my blood run cold. How could this man judge my family, and on such a trivial note at that? I went crazy in a second. The rage was already coursing through my veins, and before the inquisitive professor had time to retaliate, I was swinging the table and everything on it. My anxiety attacks had never been stronger than on that day. I grabbed my bag on the fly and took off running.

The next day, I registered for the baccalauréat as an independent candidate. I couldn't stand the childish atmosphere of the place any longer, so I simply left. I know now that I overreacted and should have swallowed my pride. But at the time, I was incapable of doing so. My parents didn't understand at all, and at first thought it was just a momentary crisis. But when they saw that I wasn't getting up in the morning, and received my confirmation of enrolment as a free candidate, they understood the seriousness of my decision. Nevertheless, they continued to wake me up every morning, shaking me to send me to school, but I wasn't going. My mother begged me to go back to school, she even cried.

- You're completely unconscious! You're going to ruin everything! Laura, please, your studies are too important to just drop them on a whim! You can't do anything without your A-levels! You can't give up, not three months before your A-levels!

I never told my parents the reason for my decision. They would have been too sad. I just shook my head and said I'd never go back. From then on, my father never spoke to me again. We didn't talk much already, but I'd just added another layer to his disappointment. Even now, I can feel when he wants to take me in his arms and tell me he loves me, but he stops himself, and walks away slowly, without saying a word.

For three months, I worked from home, learning about the courses and books on the syllabus. My mother gave me a hand, in secret from my father, who didn't approve - and never would - of my decision. In July, I passed my baccalauréat with honors. What pride I felt that day! My mother cried with joy when I told her over the phone. In the evening, my father didn't say a word either, and we ate dinner in silence, because celebrating was out of the question.

I've been very lucky, as I realize today. Is it really luck, or is it an overriding motivation and desire to succeed? At that very moment, in that amphitheater, I know that this kind of thing can't happen to me. Teachers have, as a rule, too many students to remember all the names, to consider them, and therefore insult them. Here, we work for ourselves alone.

I take several other classes during the day: translation, language lab. After five hours of classes, I head back to my cosy nest where my love is waiting for me. It's such a beautiful day, how could I be happier? I have a boyfriend who loves me and with whom I live in the center of V., I study, and even if I don't have much money, I'm in good health. What more could I ask for?

I get on the crowded subway train. I'm going to succeed this year, I know it, I feel it, I want it.

Chapter 4

The Grind

October 4, 2006

I come home exhausted from school. I finish at 8 p.m. on Wednesday evening, and then have to take the metro for about three quarters of an hour. I'm tired from the night before: I finished work at 9pm. In the car, I think of Manu, I can't wait to see him again. I think of the little dish he'll have prepared for me, and maybe he'll have set the table and put out a few candles.

Tonight, when I get home, I also know that we're going to talk about this past month together. I dread this moment because I know we have a lot on our minds that we don't talk about. Today, our life is becoming more and more like a roommate. We only see each other in the evenings, and when I get home, I gobble down a quick meal and get down to studying.

At first, Manu was content with this, sometimes making a slight pout but only saying to me:

- Go to work, you've got a job to do.

He spends the evening in front of the television, doing very little work for college. I silently exile myself to the bedroom, kissing him one last time.

Manu is one of those very few people who are naturally gifted. He excels in his field, although I've never really seen him work. I'm jealous of him sometimes, of his intelligence and his ability to handle things as they come. Me, I often work until very late at night.

Then, when he wants to go to bed, Manu comes gently into the room: this is the signal for me to go and work on the plastic table in the kitchen. Manu is already sound asleep when I join him in bed. It's my turn to lie down and fall asleep. In the morning, it's off to university or work, depending on the day of the week.

So far, I've liked this routine, because I've lived it with him. At the telemarketing company, I earn around 400 euros. I paid him the much-awaited 300 euros rent for September, pretending not to know that he was going to spend it with his mates at parties, smoking and so on. I don't have much left to finish the month, no way of having a bit of fun, doing a bit of shopping, or even going out with my friends. But I don't want to spoil anything, our story is too beautiful. I've never loved anyone as much as Manu.

But very quickly, in just one month, things turned sour. Tired of having to spend every evening in front of the TV, Manu started going out a lot, sometimes coming home at dawn. I put up with it at first, not having anything better to offer him between my books and my job. I'm also happy to keep my independence and freedom. But lately, time seems to be running out for me. Very often when I come home in the evening, Manu has already left to join his mates. I can tell whether he's been gone a long time or not: sometimes all that's left in the living room ashtray is the end of a smoking joint. He spends very little time with me. Exhausted by the pace of my life, I don't have the strength or courage to wait up for him, and almost every night I fall asleep alone in our bed. I'm often tempted to curl up on the sofa and finish his joint, but I never do. Firstly, because he might reproach me, but mainly because it would prevent me from doing my job properly.

As the days go by, Manu becomes increasingly bitter and stingy towards me. All his money goes on going out and smoking. I thought I was kidding myself at first, unable to come to terms with this reality. But the facts are there: Manu is having a very hard time with what is now just an ordinary roommate, and he makes me feel it every day. I can no longer take life as lightly as I used to under my parents' roof.

Worse still, I have the distinct impression that Manu is taunting me. He wears new clothes all the time; in short, he can afford to do everything I can't do. A gap has opened up between us, a gap that's no longer just financial, even if it was based on money to begin with. I can feel us drifting further apart every day, without being able to do anything about it.

But tonight, we're planning a romantic dinner. I've been asking him for a week now, sensing that we both need to get together. He's given in, even going so far as to offer to cook for me himself, so that all I have to do is get my feet under the table. I got a head start on my work for the week on purpose. When I left class, I put on make-up in a subway window to look pretty when I got there. Not much, just a little kohl pencil under the eyes.

As I step through the door, I sense something is wrong. The apartment is far too quiet for Manu to be there. I have to face the facts: he's not here. I inspect the kitchen, trying to convince myself that he's gone out to buy bread, but the room is empty, and there's no sign that he's started eating. My stomach is rumbling, I'm very hungry. Since I didn't have enough money to buy a sandwich for lunch, I stayed in the library to study.

I sit down in front of the TV and cry. The clock ticks and Manu doesn't come home. I try to work, but I can't concentrate. I can't even look at the TV, my retina can't print the scrolling images. Call a girlfriend? Why should I? She'll laugh at me and tell me that guys are all the same, that you can't count on them. Manu isn't like that, Manu loves me deeply and cares about me.

But midnight approaches and Manu still isn't there. I'm too proud to call him on his mobile, and I've run out of credit anyway. I've smoked all my tobacco, and the pack of rolling papers is lying on the table. Why is he doing this to me? Why to me? Don't I work hard enough as it is? After just one month, I can't take it anymore, I'm exhausted all the time, for a few extra radishes, because I can hardly see the color of my money.

Suddenly, a key turns in the lock. I hold my breath, I didn't even imagine I'd be facing Manu tonight. I quickly dry my tears with the back of my hand, I don't want to look at him like that, my make-up must have run.

The next second, Manu is in the kitchen. I stare at him, he looks at me with his eyes reddened by the joints and, quite naturally, says:

- How are you? Not studying?

My body feels like it's going to explode! He can't be serious. He's obviously stoned.

- What? Are you kidding me? Where have you been? You know I've been waiting for you all evening? Weren't we supposed to have dinner tonight?

I'm screaming, I can't control myself. I'm so tired that as the words come out of my mouth I wonder where I get all this energy.

Manu bows his head, he knows he's hurt me.

- Look, Laura, I don't know what happened, but I didn't mean to, I swear. I was in the kitchen, and I really meant to make you dinner. Then I opened the fridge and saw that you hadn't bought anything. It was your turn to go shopping, wasn't it? Yes, it was your turn and you didn't do it.

- So that's why? You decide to let me cry all night just for that? Is this your punishment for me?

- No, Laura, it's not just these races, it's everything. I know you don't have any money, but we agreed to split the expenses. Plus, I just got the gas bill today, so that just added to it.

He looks me straight in the eye and doesn't shout at all. Despite all my good will, I don't understand what he's telling me, I don't see how he dares say that to me when I'm doing everything in my power to help him financially. I've always been embarrassed to talk about money.

- And like last time, I was the one who was going to do the shopping, because otherwise we weren't going to have anything to eat. I got tired of giving in, I got tired of you relying on me all the time. So I went for a walk, to see a couple of friends, to take my mind off things…

I remain silent, I really don't see what I could add. Manu has really reached the height of his stinginess. He's asking me for money for rent, shopping and bills, which adds up to around 450 euros a month. I don't have enough on my salary, so I make up for it with the little pocket money my mother gives me each month. Not much; the little she can afford, she gives to me. For the past month, I've stopped paying the flat-rate for my phone, putting the apartment's costs at the top of my spending list. On top of that, I work fifteen hours a week in this telemarketing firm, twenty hours at college, plus the hours I spend studying. He doesn't even work, and the money his mother puts into his account each month for rent, he spends on joints and clothes, and also collects my share. In short, I don't consider myself a freeloader in this situation; I contribute and deserve this apartment just as much as he does.

But despite everything, I love him like crazy, and at this moment, I don't even hate him. He impresses me too much for me to find anything to dislike. I'm ashamed of my weakness for handsome faces with devastating eyes.

Manu finally takes me in his arms, gently, and I accept his embrace. The moment is not at all dramatic; I feel good in his arms, that's all that matters. He releases me a few minutes later, observes me with his big black eyes and suddenly says:

- Listen, I think that in future, to avoid this kind of situation, we're going to do our shopping separately, each for ourselves. It'll be easier for everyone, and we won't have any more arguments like this.

I just can't believe it. So all that's happened tonight isn't enough? He wants to add another layer?

- I beg your pardon?

- Yes, I really think it will be better for us. Besides, with our schedules, we hardly ever eat together, and we don't like the same things anyway.

I'm still not saying anything, but I'm thinking the same thing. What more can I say? I'm not going to try and convince the biggest scoundrel on earth. The mere fact that it bothers him is enough for me to understand that there's nothing I can do about it. He's cheap, he's spoiled, and he'll stay that way for a long time. But he doesn't realize the pain he's inflicting on me. My marriage is falling apart.

I nod, forcing myself to smile, but both he and I know something's wrong between us. Something to do with money. Maybe something to do with a difference in social class, which he can't stand after all. His mother often says I'm not good enough for him.

The next day, when I get home from work, he's made room for me in the cupboard where we normally put the cans.

Chapter 5

Hunger

October 26, 2006

My mother passes me the chicken dish, never taking her eyes off me. She hasn't stopped since the beginning of the meal. It's the All Saints' vacation and I'm visiting my parents for two or three days, though I haven't yet decided exactly how long I'll be staying. We're sitting at the table with my mother, my mute father and my sister, who can't stop talking.

- It's good chicken, isn't it, Laura?" said my mother.

I know she's not taking her eyes off my movements: I sink my fork into a beautiful thigh, and using my other hand, I grab it to devour it like an ogre. I'm eating like four today, I'm really hungry. This dinner is without doubt the biggest feast I've had in a month.

- Yes, it's delicious, I love it.

My sister is the only one who makes conversation, and I'm the only one who really listens to her. I know that my presence interferes with my father's thoughts. He doesn't talk much already, but when I'm around, he's as dumb as a post.

Our relationship has always been difficult, we've always loved each other, but in silence. My father is someone who commands respect. At the age of twenty, he left his native Spain to escape dictatorship and poverty and try his luck in France. He was brought up in a very strict family, which pays a great deal of attention to respecting tradition. He has always maintained this natural coldness towards us daughters, especially towards me, just as his father had done before with his children. I've always accepted it, because it's the way he works.

I know he loves me, but he's never told me, never put his feelings into words. I'm the eldest, and I know I was a much-wanted child. My parents spoiled me a lot in my early childhood. But as I grew up and my relationship with my mother became closer and closer, my father became more and more mute, probably not knowing how to deal with his daughter. The aplomb I displayed when he wanted to punish me seemed abnormal, disrespectful. Little by little, he locked himself in a bubble that amounted to ignoring me. Whenever I'm in the room, he only talks to me about the really essential things. I know I've disappointed him on several occasions with my behavior. The high point came when I dropped out of my final year. My sister and I always knew that there were family preferences: I was my mother's, she was my father's. But we couldn't help it. But there was nothing we could do about it, and accepting the obvious allowed us to avoid resentment and jealousy.

I remember one day when I was 16, I was away from home for a month. We were in the living room with my parents and sister, and I was looking at the sofa we were sitting on. It was a very old green fabric sofa, which I'd always seen at home. It was so old that my mother had once decided, when I was still a baby, to dye it dark red, to hide its obvious wear and tear. As I listened to the TV, I scratched a spot on the armrest where the dye had never set.

I suddenly blurted out:

- Maybe we should paint it green again. It's been red for a long time now and needs a facelift.

My father replied, without giving me a glance:

- This sofa has never been green.

His tone was dry and contemptuous, as if I were telling him the most idiotic story he'd ever heard.

- Of course I do, Dad, I still remember when Mom dyed it.

- This sofa has never been green, I tell you.

For a few minutes, I tried to prove to him that it was true, that I remembered it very well. I even threw myself into the photo albums to find proof of what I was saying. Seeing me rummaging through the shelves in the living room, my father flew into a frenzy of unjustified rage.

- Ah, you always have to be right! You always have to be the smart-ass, the know-it-all!

He was screaming. My mother and sister stared at him, transfixed. I didn't move either, not knowing what to do, photo album in hand.

- I'm getting fed up with you, your manners, your behavior. You're disrespectful of others, everything revolves around you, your little navel. In fact, I can't stand you anymore, you're just a… a piece of shit! That's it, a piece of shit!

He dropped the word in a whisper and left for the kitchen. My sister screamed when she heard him. My father in all his glory, my father who doesn't beat around the bush. But still, it rasped in my throat. My fists clenched and I took off running, while my mother got up and was already trying to hold me back. I grabbed my bag on the fly. My mother cried, begging me not to leave, my sister clung to my arm. My father didn't move from the kitchen.

- Mom, I can't, I can't anymore. Look how he is, it's unbearable. I'm leaving.

- But to go where? How are you going to do it?

- I'll figure it out.

And I found it. For a month, I lived with a friend and her parents. They didn't try too hard to understand, just gave me a little space in their house, which was big. I went to school with my friend every morning, and once a week I phoned my mother to give her news.

I came back after a month, not wanting to take any more advantage of the kindness of my friend and her parents. When I returned, my father ignored me, as usual. He even continued to ignore me when the affair died down. I suffered terribly, but didn't know what to do to tell him or show him. I found out later that he'd had tears in his eyes the day I left.

The situation we now find ourselves in, on this All Saints' Day, is therefore not exceptional. My sister is talking at the table, trying to break the silence that embarrasses her. Then she tires of doing all the talking and stops. We finish our meal in silence.

My mother takes me aside in the evening. I know she's wanted to talk to me ever since I arrived.

- Laura, tell me, are you eating well?

- Yes, Mum, you saw it, I've had chicken twice tonight!

- No, Laura, I'm not talking about that. Do you eat well at home? Do you and Manu have enough to eat?

So she noticed the obvious. I've lost a lot of weight in the last month, since Manu and I have our own food cupboard. I weighed over 60 kilos at the beginning of September, I was even a bit overweight, and now I'm down to 50. I come home late at night, tired, often with no time to prepare food for myself because I have to study. I run around all day, between college, the library, my job and the apartment. I've got nothing in my cupboard anyway, apart from a half-used packet of pasta that's been lying around for two weeks. I often don't eat lunch in college, and a sandwich ends up weighing me down at the end of the week. By not eating, I don't really feel hungry anymore. Well, almost.

As for Manu, he often eats out with his friends. I suppose he uses the money from my share of the rent to treat himself while I'm immersed in my books. Apart from that, we get on pretty well, with no real arguments. After all, we hardly see each other. Yet I still love him with all my might, even when I open the food cupboard and drool with envy over his tin of pâté or his pesto sauces that would make my pasta so much more appetizing.

One day, I took him a slice of Italian ham, thinking he wouldn't notice. Unfortunately, he must be counting them, as he spotted the theft straight away. I apologized at length, just telling him I was hungry and would buy him some more. Which I did the very next day, snapping up my 5 euro bill that was supposed to last me three days. I could have pushed the vice so far as to give him back just one slice, perhaps he would have realized the stupidity of his behavior. But I'm not interested in playing his game.

I definitely can't tell my mother about all this, she'd freak out and call Manu names. She'd force me to come home, which is absolutely out of the question.

- Don't worry, Mom, everything's fine.

- You'd tell me if something was wrong, wouldn't you?

- Yes, Mom, of course! Don't you worry.

She looks at me with an eye that says a lot about her skepticism. She doesn't believe me, but she can't do anything unless I tell her the truth.

Two days later, when I left my parents' house, my mother gave me a whole bag full of victuals. She winked at me as she handed it to me.

- Go home safely, darling, and take care of yourself.

My father waved, but didn't kiss me. We haven't kissed for years now.

Chapter 6

Shame

November 16, 2006

In front of the Crous building, I hesitate to enter. I'm not really sure I want to go there anymore. I stand back, not completely in front of the door.

It's November and freezing. My weight loss has accelerated dramatically in recent months. I feel as if the cold is piercing me like never before. And yet, this morning, I layered my clothes well. Since I've become so thin, I'm always cold. I shiver everywhere, even indoors: in class, at work and at home.

Winter is fast approaching and we still haven't turned on the heating in the apartment. At least, *I don't* want to. Manu turns it on as soon as he comes in, before curling up like a pacha on the sofa. I wait for him to leave and then turn it off. I've been doing this since I had to pay some of the bills. Electricity, water and heating, that's a lot together! Manu doesn't care, since he's not the one who manages these expenses. So he turns up the heat while I turn it down on the sly, unable to ask him for the favor.

At first, I studied in my normal clothes, but I soon realized that sitting in a chair for several hours without moving made me feel the cold almost as if I were outside. So now, to work, I put on a real suit: a huge scarf knitted by my mother, a fleece sports jacket and big knee-high socks. Manu laughed the first time he saw me like this, and so did I for a few seconds when I looked in the mirror. After all, there's nothing funny about the situation. I've finally got used to this extra weight on my frail shoulders, and saving money is what motivates me. I'd rather look like a high-altitude explorer than have to pay 50 euros for a bill that could be avoided.

I save all the money I can. No unnecessary expenses. Needless to say, I stopped shopping a long time ago. Firstly, I don't have the time. Anyway, what's the point of drooling over something I'll never own? So I don't tempt the devil and carefully avoid window shopping. I've finally got it into my head that I'll never wear the latest fashions. Sure, sometimes I'm envious of my college mates' new raw jeans, fitted jackets and expensive shoes. I can just stare at them, to the point of embarrassment, sigh, and then get back to my sheep. I'd like to be strong enough to say that I can't stand any consumer society and that it disgusts me, but let's be honest: who doesn't have desires and who wouldn't be tempted by them? I'm young, advertising is everywhere: I'd be perfect prey if I had money.

I envy those girls around me in the classroom. Fresh and rested, some of them have never had to work to survive financially. Their parents earn more than enough to support them. Sometimes, they have to go shopping with their mother and show their envy with a studied pout at a piece of clothing in a store, to which their mother responds by pulling out a credit card. I can't say I blame them - I'd do the same thing in a heartbeat. I just envy them their peace of mind, while for my part, I shudder at the sight of a ticket inspector in the metro, and I'm constantly wondering how I'm going to get through the month. I shudder when Manu casually asks me to pay my share of the rent. Am I the only one going through this? All these situations are so shameful, I can't talk about them to my student friends. How could they understand? So I kindly decline their invitation to lunch and lock myself away in the only free thing I have left: studying.

This wouldn't really be a problem if I had enough to eat. The state of my food cupboard is as sad as ever, and my mother's victuals haven't lasted long. Pasta, pasta and always pasta. I look at them as I prepare food, and I feel as if they're taunting me, as if to remind me that tonight, once again, I won't have anything better. At first, I accompanied them with canned tomato sauce, but a nocturnal indigestion has since disgusted me with it, and the mere idea of seeing pasta bathed in cheap sauce makes me nauseous. "With butter, it's not so bad after all."

There's also a jar of Nutella, my little piece of happiness. I don't eat more than a spoonful each time, to keep it as long as possible. It comforts me when I open the cupboard.

I was so hungry that I stopped eating. I realized that, after a while, the end comes, and the human cycle resumes on its own. After a few days on this diet, I don't really feel any pain anymore. I've got into the habit of skipping breakfast and going through my college days with nothing in my stomach. Sometimes he makes strange noises during class, but I'm so used to their presence that I don't really hear them anymore.

A girl in my class turned to my table and handed me a chocolate bar, gently mocking me:

- Here, eat something. All we can hear is your stomach rumbling!

Ashamed, I thanked her with my lips, trying to pretend that I was very amused by her joke. But I wasn't laughing at all. Slowly, in silence, I savored the chocolate bar. If I'd been anywhere else, I'd have devoured it in a matter of seconds, it was so tempting. I restrained myself, dignified, but I still retrieved the last crumbs from my notebook with my finger. I would have eaten another.

In the evening, when I find the time or strength to eat on my way home from university or work, I swallow a bowl of rice pudding. And if I want to cheer myself up, a spoonful of Nutella at the end of my "meal". It certainly sounds sad, but this chocolate acts like a tranquillizer. I lick the spoon clean, to get the most out of the taste, right to the end. I have the impression that I work better afterwards.

Then, one lunchtime, what was supposed to happen happened. I collapsed in the middle of class. Pulling too hard on the rope, I didn't realize that I'd exceeded all the limits my body could bear. People started to panic a bit, but I soon came to my senses and started working again. Some people insisted that I go to the college infirmary, which I politely refused. I don't need a doctor to know what I'm suffering from. I suffer from not having any money.

That was the day I decided to go to the Crous to find a solution, some financial help. The lack of money is playing havoc with my health and I don't feel ready to accept this reality. I'm revolted that I have to struggle so much to eat, to eat in order to be able to work. But once I'm in front of the building, I don't have the strength to go in. I never imagined I'd end up at the Crous for such a reason. I know a lot of students go there to ask for help, but it's not in my character. For me, coming here is synonymous with defeat: I couldn't manage on my own. But let's face it. I can't manage on my own, I need a little help. This situation of perpetual starvation is no longer possible.

So I enter the building and kindly wait at the reception desk. Half an hour later, I'm greeted by a lady who has just seen a crowd of students. In her office, I beat around the bush.

- I've come to see you because I'm having serious financial difficulties and I wanted to know if I could get help from your organization.

In a split second, I recount my life without money, Manu and the rent, my difficulties, the lack that is felt every day. I take the opportunity to observe her. She listens attentively and seems concerned by my story. She's young, in her thirties, and probably remembers her own penniless college years.

After a good fifteen minutes of explanations, I finally shut up, but my silence awaiting an answer from her makes her cough.

- All I can offer at the moment are meal vouchers for your meals at Crous. They're really cheap, with a meal costing less than 3 euros!

I do a quick calculation in my head. I can't spend nearly 15 euros a week on just one meal a day. I came here hoping to be offered significant discounts for lunch AND dinner.

- That's a small weekly amount for me. I wanted to know if you had any other solutions.

- In your case, I can only think of one way not to spend money on food: Restos du Cœur.

She said it slowly, very gently, aware of the psychological impact it would have on me. It didn't fail. I look at her with wide eyes. Now, in one sentence, I'm at the very bottom of the French social ladder. So low that I can't afford my meals, so low that I'm offered food given to the homeless. I think I'm dreaming, I can't believe she's serious. But she keeps looking at me, with big, understanding eyes.

I mumble a vague thank you and ask where I need to go to find the Restos du Coeur. On a piece of paper, she scribbles an address in beautiful handwriting. She applies herself, perhaps to prove that she's touched by my Cosette story. I greet her quickly, eager to get it over with. She shakes my hand warmly in the corridor before shouting "next" in a shrill voice.

I face the November cold again as I leave the building. With the small piece of paper in hand, I walk quickly to warm up. I'm not going, it's out of the question. I can't bring myself to go to this place; I tell myself I don't need it all that much, after all. I almost feel like I'm "stealing" this food from these poor people who really have nothing. Above all, I can't relate to them, the homeless. I have a roof over my head, a job and I'm studying. No, I've made up my mind, I'm happy with my pasta after all. After all, I'm not the first and I won't be the last.

Chapter 7

The End

December 9, 2006

In every life, there's a night when you mature too quickly. Nothing will ever be the same again. Farewell to innocence. It's one of those melancholy nights when balance sheets hurt. In this case, mine is financial. No money, bills begging, a flat to pay. Plunged into the dark, leaning back in my chair in front of Manu's computer screen, I can barely control my finger as it frantically scrolls over the mouse in search of a solution. One ad site, then another. A window, more or less hidden towards the bottom of the page and intended to be discreet, catches my eye: reserved for those over 18. Two categories: "venal" or not. Right away, I'm tempted to choose the second, as if to justify myself to someone. But the room is empty and I'm alone. Let's be honest, money is clearly the main reason I'm on this site. *Just out of curiosity*, I tell myself, knowing full well that the line has just been crossed. No special protection, I click (over 18, my ass!). In the "keyword" box, I enter my student status and city.

An exhaustive list of applicants appears, which I scroll down with my mouse. So it's possible and so easy? I scroll through the ads, which, after a quick glance, all look the same. The same words are repeated over and over again: "girl", "tender moments", "meeting", "looking for". I'm looking for money too, and fast. Stupidly categorized under the more than dubious alibi of "massage", the men who show up are on average well into their fifties. Older than my own father. *Dad, if you only knew…* The major difference is that they have dough, lots of it, and seem willing to spend it on a fantasy I'm potentially capable of fulfilling. The rates, when they are mentioned, speak of hundreds of euros per hour. Is this possible? All these figures conjure up my desire for possession in the space of a second. I'm already imagining myself with all that dough in my battered wallet, sticking out everywhere! They also speak of several hours in their company. Anyway, one afternoon in a lifetime, I guess, when you really need money, isn't much. Maybe that's my solution, the one I've been waiting for. Comfort, and fast.

I've done without these comforts until now, quite well in fact. My parents' apartment in a council estate until I was 18, the simplest of clothes, rolled cigarettes, all of which suited me just fine. Until now. Of course, I was sometimes envious, like everyone else, but I'd never really been materialistic, perhaps for lack of means. Never a penny in my pockets, forced to cheat on transport, a vaguely bearable life. Sometimes inconvenient, often embarrassing when it came time to pay the bill, but you get used to it. I tell myself that "massages" would easily afford me the luxury of choice. What I don't realize is that precisely the opposite is happening: I'll never have a choice again.

Mixed with the dark night, often the source of insane acts, my senses were stirred into a mad ebullition. The sight, at first, vicious and so present at every moment. The sight of those bills I've been refusing to open for a week, abandoned on the modest wooden cabinet in the living room that serves as my library; the sight of the bills handed to me by my few friends to pay for my umpteenth coffee at the local bistro. A hypothesis takes shape, which had certainly been latent all these years: with money, not only could I study all the time, but I'd like myself better.

I'm a little delirious. My whole body is crying out for this possible abundance, I can almost feel it on my fingertips. All I have to do is move my finger on the mouse, just that, a tiny pressure. My hand becomes uncontrollable, guided by this dark desire so taboo and paradoxically so sparkling. My arms, my head, my whole being knows that at the end of my hand lies a solution, as controversial as it may be, a way to solve everything, at least for now. My whole organism joins forces against my feeble wisdom, in a hurry to get it over with. Never mind the rest, we'll see.

A frenzy suddenly took hold of me. It's already too late. One look at these messages and I'm completely in their hands. *Don't think, Laura, just type those damn messages and you'll get out of the mess you're in; it's the only solution and you know it.* Don't back down in the face of fear, a way is offered to me, I jump on it. I'm a go-getter who can't tell good from bad, and I'm desperate to get out of anything, whatever the cost. I've been schizophrenic ever since. Reading those ads split me in two: there's the Laura who's fully aware that she's playing with fire, and the money-hungry Laura. A ridiculous challenge is added: I can do it, I'll prove it to myself. So I type, I type on my keyboard as if I were typing on my own life, as if to eradicate this lack that has grown inside me a little more every day. I believe myself to be the mistress of my reason, already in perdition, I believe myself to be invincible with the promise of this money alone.

Manu isn't here, so take advantage. I do glance at the time and the front door, just in case. He's still with his friends at the moment, so he won't be back just yet.

I type quickly, without taking the time to think, so as not to imagine the world I'm venturing into. I fell; yes, in five minutes I fell. After an hour, my hand stopped, satisfied. Some forty replies were sent in my madness. A vague number corresponding to people who, for the moment, don't really exist. The blurred image they convey through their words means nothing to me. The feeling that this was all a dream never left me. I was careful not to think while my fingers played on the keyboard. Then, to cut the reverie short, I quickly lowered the screen and went for a walk.

The night was enough. From the very first hour, the notion of lacking and needing other people arose, in parallel with my own. In a way, they and I are alike: we're all in need of something. Perhaps I wasn't dreaming, in fact; my mailbox is already showing the consequences of my actions, actions I can no longer control, even in the safety of my own home.

I replied, lost in a trance of need, desperate to find the fucking money, and now I'm faced with my own bullshit. The student turns on the mature male, I have the proof now. They want their fantasies fulfilled, and I want mine.

You always remember your first message. For me, it's Joe, a strange nickname with which he signs the e-mails he sends me. Joe, better known as Joseph. The use of a pseudonym seemed obvious to him; on the one hand, to look younger and trendier in the eyes of his future collaborators, and on the other, to avoid exposing himself too much. Does he also split into two when the night comes and he feels desire rising? I didn't try to find a pseudonym. Too complete, too much of a novice, I didn't ask myself the question. I just think that Laura will always be Laura, whatever happens.

Young man, 50, seeks occasional masseuse. Female students welcome.

His message is oddly courteous, but reading through the lines, you can feel his being sweating with envy. He asks me if I have any taboos. These words scream at me not to have any, that the payoff will only be better. He didn't ask for a photograph, but sent me one. He's 57 years old. You can imagine what he looks like. Reality strikes now, hard and intractable, forcing me to become aware.

For the first time in my life, when I read his message, I feel more childish than ever, me who has always been ahead of my age. This man is mature, three times my age. He's expressing well-considered fantasies that we're guessing are buried and poorly denied. He's looking for a candid girl, probably in a short pleated skirt, English socks, enjoying a strawberry

The End

lollipop. Then he turns off his computer, because his wife has just entered the room, asking him to join her and her daughter for dinner. And during the meal, he acts as if nothing had happened, because he's been hiding all this from them for years now.

Perhaps he'd glance at his daughter, older than the girl in the skirt, and think she was pretty and had a bright future. When she asks him to pass her the plate, he'll do so with a smile. In the evening, at best, he makes love to his wife, politely, taking his time, holding back to give her time to enjoy herself. Because he loves her. Because he loves them both, from the depths of his heart.

The question of rates came up, of course, and I got burned all by myself. Behind the screen, where lies are so common and so easy to conceal, it was easy for me to get under the skin of a professional prostitute, who's done her homework and doesn't take it easy. But when the time came to talk money, I failed. Spontaneously, I wanted a thousand and one, but I thought it wouldn't be credible. With time, I'm going to learn that there's nothing to be lost by daring and setting the bar very high, even if it means renegotiating afterwards in the face of too much reluctance.

These men imagine, and in my case - I must admit - rightly so, that if a girl asks for a lot, it must be worth it. An outrageous amount of money often heralds a pleasant surprise: perhaps a gorgeous girl who, because of her looks, can afford to force her prices. Ass for cash, occasionally. They probably think that these are girls who like sex, who want more of it, naughty students who want mature men to take charge of their monotonous sex lives, to change them from the dumb pussies of their age.

My inexperience led me to offer 100 euros an hour, based on what I'd read in the other ads. The famous Joe looked delighted, as he probably didn't expect anything of the sort. It was also certainly at that moment that he realized he was dealing with a novice. In the back of his mind, he had undoubtedly already come up with a few scenarios, pushing back the limits that had always been imposed on him by the "pros".

The two of us set up a meeting after a few short e-mail exchanges, in which I pretended to participate. We'd meet in three days, in a hotel near the station. He'd be wearing a red polo shirt so I'd recognize him, because even though I have his photograph, he didn't want to miss me, or go out of his way for nothing. He was very insistent on the fact that he doesn't live in the city, and that he'd be very disappointed if I didn't show up after a long walk. He really talks to me like a kid you warn when you realize she's about to do something stupid.

I said "yes" without further ado, to get the subject off my mind more quickly. But even so, the details are already falling into place. A patchwork is gradually taking shape in my head. In my imagination, I take his face, associate it with the body of a man in his sixties, wearing a red polo shirt. I place it in front of a shabby hotel on the street leading to the station, a street notorious for its prostitutes and drug dealing.

Once I've closed the computer and extinguished the last embers of my reverie, I resume my mundane life in an instant. Manu's still not here, the idiot. I decide to immerse myself in

The End

a Spanish translation exercise. But I can't concentrate. After several minutes' thought, I managed to persuade myself not to go to the appointment under any circumstances. I've played with fire a little, even to the point of burning my fingertips, but at no point am I seriously thinking of going. Joe will be alone in front of the hotel, and I'll stay at home.

Yet this silly figure keeps coming up: 100 euros an hour. Three days of waiting. Waiting for what? I've decided not to go, so why did I even bother to keep my promise to this stranger? I'm not going, period, end of story. My thoughts wander, between reason and need, careful to avoid my young heart, which has no place in this story.

I look at my food cupboard, empty. I glance stupidly at my bills on the cabinet. My head aches. I snap my translation book shut.

Once, no more.

Chapter 8

The Sucker

December 12, 2006

Only three days have passed since our e-mail exchanges. It's not so bad after all. This way, I don't have time to think about what I'm doing, and I need the money too much. We agreed to meet at 2 p.m., for an hour valued at 100 euros. Just one hour, before I leave for my telemarketing job. Until the last minute, I don't know if I'm really going. But the pocket-hole syndrome naturally guided my steps.

Without really knowing why or how, I found myself heading towards this famous street, walking as one does towards an appointment that you haven't written down in your diary, but which you can't forget. I've forced myself to pretend that I'm neglecting this appointment by putting on a pair of jeans and a cardigan. But underneath my outfit, which I wanted to be basic in case I bumped into someone I knew along the way, no one could guess that I was wearing itchy stockings. I laughed when I put them on, feeling a bit ridiculous in them. I even shaved in the shower this morning. Of course, this happens to me a lot, especially since I've been living with Manu, but this time I really applied myself, going over my knee and ankles several times. Ankles are a very delicate area. I want to please and make a good impression. The reasons for this painstaking work are not yet entirely clear.

I realize as I go that I haven't prepared any explanations if I meet someone in the street. I'm a good liar, I'll find something to invent. Once I'm near the station, I hurry on. The sooner I get there, the sooner I'll be done.

My head methodically lists the rules I'm going to make myself respect: once, no more. I should have smoked a joint before I left. Why didn't I think of that? I would have been much more zen, more relaxed, I would have enjoyed the situation eventually. Eventually.

I've strangely taken certain precautions that seem necessary: I won't show up first, I'll wait for him to arrive first. Deep down, I still think this is a joke. Stationed in front of the hotel, I wait in the December cold, watching the pedestrians, almost hoping that Joe will arrive so I don't have to endure the icy wind. Joe, the draft that will become reality a few moments later.

A host of questions came to me, quite logically. He told me he'd booked a room. Did he give his real name at reception? I didn't say anything when he suggested such a place, but I find it such a dismal choice. He must test all his new conquests there, and if they deserve it, he makes them dream the next time by taking them to more suitable places. But after all, if it's just ass he wants, why bother? For all we know, he's already got his own account there.

A hair's breadth ahead of schedule, a man of a certain age stops in front of the building, quietly looking around as if nothing had happened. "A man of a certain age" is what you say when you're polite and don't want to say the word "old". So, in short, he's old. I never imagined I'd sleep with a man that age one day.

He looks nothing like the photo. Despite a younger, sportier look, he looks 57. He wears a red-checked shirt, jogging pants and sneakers; graying hair accompanies his age. A large, still-brown moustache adorns the center of his face. No real style, but at least he's clean-cut. Someone I'd obviously never turn my back on in the street, but not someone with an off-putting appearance either. And to think I'm going to see this guy naked! And to think he's going to want to touch me! I shudder with disgust. Maybe it's because I was expecting so much worse that I leapt out of my hiding place to cross the street and join him. I also think I'm already forcing myself to stop thinking.

He saw me coming and his face changed expression. I couldn't tell if it was good or bad. We kissed promptly, both of us obviously a little stressed. But then his demeanor suddenly relaxed, and he introduced himself very courteously, in a soft voice. My God, he's so old! Ah yes, now his 57 years were clear.

- Hello, Laura," he says, watching me.

- Hello, Joe," I said, without knowing what else to say.

I couldn't help but ogle him up and down, without any embarrassment. I don't feel particularly moved, more hateful, I confess. His accent struck me and triggered in me this need

The Sucker

to inspect him: he exudes the country bumpkin. His into-
nations, his voice that sings at the end of sentences: he's the
perfect representative of the country boy exiled to the "big
city" to make a career, but who's never been able to fully shake
off his origins. At this point, I wonder if he's really going to
pay me. Given his basic, if not too *cheap,* get-up, I'm entitled
to wonder.

His posture betrays a certain routine; it's clearly not his
first time. He's obviously delighted with my appearance.
I pretend not to notice that he's staring at me with eyes like
fried whiting. For him, my arrival is a gift from heaven: what
could be better? A student, offering her body for the first
time, and what's more, at ridiculously low rates. He shudders
in anticipation and congratulates himself on his wise choice.

For my part, I glance around frantically. I've had this
immeasurable fear since the moment I found him. I'm desperate to get in, because the only thing I fear at the moment is
that someone will recognize me. He must have understood,
judging by my slightly tense face; he opened the way. He
must have understood a lot, seeing me for the first time on
this sidewalk.

I slipped in behind him through the front door. I could tell
by the way he acted that he knew the ropes.

I walk politely behind him, as if to hide. I don't think I want
to see the look on the receptionist's face. He's not fooled; he
understands perfectly well what's going on and that this room
booked in the middle of the afternoon isn't going to accom-
modate tourists who've just disembarked from the train, tired
from their journey.

I hid so well that I didn't notice the gendarmes right away: Joe didn't slow down or twitch at the sight of them, in short, no sign to alert me. And yet there they were: two or three heads wearing kepi chatting at the reception desk. Now that I'm face to face with them, I would have preferred the accusing gaze of the unknown guard.

But I suddenly realize that I don't give a shit about the receptionist and that what might happen in the next few seconds might have a much bigger impact on my life. Gendarmes can land you in jail.

Once in front of them, I look down in panic. A heat I know well, the kind that physically warns me that danger is near, has invaded my belly and is now torturing my guts. This is it, it's over before it's begun. This is it, I'm not 20 and I'm going to get caught for a vulgar game whose consequences I haven't measured. As I walk along, I unroll a Hollywood movie in my head. I see myself at the police station, with a blinding white light in my face, handcuffed, gesticulating my innocence on an iron chair. And then my parents summoned to the local police station, my mother in tears of course, and my father not giving me a glance because I've soiled the family name. What a nightmare!

I walk on, knowing that in a tenth of a second a gendarme will arrest me. Still, I keep on walking, following the man responsible for this whole affair, for my future life as a prostitute. Let's talk about him! Joe doesn't seem to give a damn about what's going on around him. The cops are going to get us!

Yet I don't scream, no sound comes out of my tetanized mouth. Wait a second: if the animal doesn't blink, maybe it's in on it too! What if it's an undercover cop? I've been ripped off like a fool…

I'm still hating myself and the world when I realize we're already in the elevator. He hasn't even suggested we split up and meet in the bedroom, which would have betrayed some fear, very logical in itself. In fact, he couldn't care less about chickens. It all makes sense a few minutes later, when something incredible happens: nothing. Absolutely nothing. The gendarmes saw us, it's obvious, we brushed past them as we walked. But nothing happened.

Instead, we continued the elevator ride in silence, him probably already fantasizing about what he's going to do to me once we get to the top; and me, barely over the head-on collision with the gendarmes, petrified. Once upstairs, he made his way to the room without a moment's hesitation - he must know the hotel like the back of his hand.

In a hurry, he turned the key in the lock, passing me in front like a pseudo-gentleman. I entered the room with a step that gave the impression of having made up my mind. The sooner it's done, the sooner it's over.

The first thing I saw were the filthy, faded-green curtains covering the two windows. What a horrible decoration! Who has bad enough taste to put up curtains like that in a room like this? The rest is basic. Quite large, but with the bare essentials: a bed and matching bedside tables, a table set against the wall with a telephone. It's a good thing I'm able to spot it right away, so I can pounce on it if Joe gets violent. The carpet is plain, a very dark blue, almost black, I can't remember exactly.

A click of the lock snaps me out of my thoughts. Joe has locked the door. Out of the question! We still haven't exchanged a word, at least other than introductory banalities.

- No, it's not. The door stays open, I say.

What an affront! As soon as I've said these words, I realize I've used a harsh tone. Is it proper to be so categorical in front of a guy to whom you have to give your all? I don't realize it at the time. That's the real Laura talking, the one who says what she thinks. He made a little pout, just for a second but long enough for me to perceive it.

- Suit yourself. It was just to keep the peace.

He doesn't upset me and respects my demands. Maybe it won't be so hard after all.

Excited and so uncomfortable, I can't stop moving back and forth between the few pieces of furniture, as if to relieve my stress.

- Are you feeling well?" he asks.

My tension is so palpable that the old man feels obliged to check up on me.

- Yes, I'm fine, just fine," I said quickly, to get rid of this superfluous conversation.

- So, you're a student? Studying what? Exactly how old are you?

I can't answer. I'm too confused and too busy looking at him. His body is rather athletic, and apart from his vomit-inducing shirt, the rest is very passable. He impresses me, in a way, with his mature age.

He continues to ask me a couple of uninteresting questions, which I don't answer either, more out of discomfort than rudeness.

I turn around, and my gaze falls again on the ugly curtains. Why am I so obsessed with them? Everything about them disgusts me. They taunt me with their unwashed fabric. I realize that if they bother me so much, it must be because they remind me of my miserable, ugly situation.

He crosses the room with a black briefcase in his hand that I didn't notice before. A real businessman's briefcase. He quietly placed it on the end of the bed, starting to play with the mechanism to open it. A truly incongruous scene: just imagine this guy going all professional in his lumberjack plaid shirt!

But what could he be hiding in there? I give him an inquisitive look. I'm now expecting him to bring out a real doctor's kit, complete with tools and utensils for butchering me. Or maybe just a little gadget to spice up our encounter. Suddenly I'm anxious to know what he's capable of - after all, I don't know him from Adam or Eve.

The briefcase lies open on the bed. For a moment, I think I'm in a Tarantino movie, and as I get closer to see the contents, I even imagine wads of cash. Instead, Joe hands me an ordinary letter.

- What do you want me to do? Read it here in front of you?

Still without speaking, he nods at me. He's certainly not original, but he's desperate to create an enigmatic situation. In the end, I have to admit, it works. Confused, I take the piece of paper in my hands. His handwriting is diligent, and you can tell from the very first lines that he's taken great care to choose his words carefully.

Hello, Laura

First of all, I was pleased with your punctuality and I thank you for it.

What a madman! Would he have written another letter if I'd been late?

Today we're going to play together. I want you to read my letter all the way through, and then do it as you go along. First, I want you to undress completely.

Time has now turned into a gigantic, awkward silence. Joe has fallen silent and waits, arms folded. A real job interview. If I pass the nudity test, I'm sure to be hired.

I slowly place the letter on the edge of the bed. Without thinking, I take off my top and, without waiting for any reaction from him, slide my jeans down my thighs. I bend down in a movement that I want to be languorous, to free myself completely.

Joe is staring at me with his mouth open. You can see the beginnings of an erection under his jogging suit.

My bra, Petit Bateau panties and stockings are now the only things covering my anatomy. Standing in front of him, hands behind my back, I present him with all my intimacy. I'm the child-woman, Nabokov's Lolita, and he loves it. I'm disconnected from all reality. A real torture begins for me, which I exorcise by giggling. I'm so self-conscious about my body, despite its slight shape, and the situation is truly destabilizing. He doesn't move; his silence has lasted for fifteen minutes now.

He takes a long breath and his lips begin to open. Come on, say something.

- Whoa!" he shrieks.

And that's all there is to it. Just an onomatopoeia. No one can understand how I suddenly feel. My body suddenly swells with hope and contentment. This guy, whom I don't know from nowhere, has succeeded in one word and a split second where dozens of others have failed: making me realize that my body is pleasant. Why did it have to be him? I have no answer, it's simply inexplicable. All I know is that for the first time, I heard and accepted a compliment. At that second, I saw him as a man and no longer as the fat, disgusting creep who wants to get his paws all over me. The girls must have flocked to him, and yet, he still manages to be impressed.

We exchange a knowing smile, and something eerily close to trust is established between us.

- This is exactly why I don't like "professionals" - they can't have the innocent look you have.

I don't really know how to take that remark. Does he already consider me a prostitute? Is one or two passes enough to merit that word?

With his chin, he pointed to the letter again, for me to continue reading. I do so.

Now I want you to go and take a shower, and I'll take one after you. I'm really glad you came and that we're spending this time together.

I skim the rest of the letter. After all, it's obvious what's coming next: naked, in the shower, I've a sneaking suspicion we're not about to start a frenzied game of Scrabble.

Thank you, Laura, for coming today. I'm delighted to meet you and I hope we'll see each other again. You seem like a nice person.

A good person? How can he know? Am I a good person because I'm willing to strip down to my underwear in front of him for money I don't have? The letter ends with blah, blah. Nevertheless, his words betray a kindness I could never have imagined. The appointment doesn't turn out as planned. I thought it was going to be a mindless hour, where I'd put my brain aside, but I end up thinking about this guy!

I remove the slight superfluity of fabric I still have and obediently head for the bathroom.

Once I'd closed the door, I faced the mirror in the cramped room. Despite all my efforts, I couldn't avoid her reflection. Naked, in front of the mirror, I'm suddenly tempted to fall into melancholy. I'm disconnected once again from this "session", as I come face to face with myself, with what I'm doing. I've never really looked at myself so closely and attentively. I'm strangely proud of my body after Joe's onomatopoeia, and begin to examine myself. I've never really liked my belly, but right now I'm looking at it differently. Still, there's this voice deep inside me trying to call me to my senses. Shit, I'm becoming completely panicked, tortured between two opposing feelings.

The shower requirement had marked a pause in the adventure, a pause that forced me to really think. To cut a long story short, I turn on the water and adjust the pressure.

Incongruous as it may seem, I'm smiling, yes. Because I suddenly find myself pretty. I've fallen back into childhood, and the compliment from this man, older than my own father, has filled me like that of a grandfather to his granddaughter.

The water runs slowly over my body, which I frantically soap with the cheap soap courtesy of the hotel. There's no reason for me to scrub so hard; he hasn't touched me yet. But I keep going back and forth, scrubbing myself to death. Maybe I'm washing myself of the situation, of him, of the room, of his compliments, of the green curtains.

Once I'm clean, I grab a towel to dry off, which I wedge cleverly into the hollow of my breasts, panicking at the thought of him entering the bathroom. I hesitate for a second. I don't know whether to go out naked or not. Even as I ask myself this question, I realize that at some point I'll be naked in front of him. It might as well be me he's decided. My hand grabs the knot on my chest and loosens it. The towel falls limply to the floor with a thud.

When I open the door, Joe is on the bed in his boxers. I see his torso for the first time. No surprise, he's 57, with white hair and a slight paunch on his belly.

- You excite me enormously, you know?" he says with a sigh.

Yes, I can imagine that.

- So here's how it's going to work.

He pauses.

- I'm someone who loves staging. I fantasize a lot about it," he says quietly.

Seeing my slightly disconcerted look, he then hastens to explain.

- Now, I want you to leave the room, wait in the hallway for a moment and knock twice on the door. When I tell you to come in, you will come in and do as I ask.

- What, like this? Naked?

- Yes, like that, naked.

Don't you want a hundred bucks too? At the rate things are going, I'll end up paying for it! The fantasy of the naked girl knocking on the door is too much. What would happen if someone saw me? I'm losing my nerve.

- No.

- What do you mean, no? Why not?

- No.

- Can you tell us why?

His gaze suddenly changed. I can tell by the sound of his voice that my refusal has shattered the sexy image he was building up. He senses that I can put a stop to his lascivious inventions, and even though I'm polite and well-groomed, he doesn't seem ready to accept it.

I get scared at that moment. I've broken his rules. I tell myself that he won't give up on his goal if I don't keep up.

- Because it's hard for me. Getting undressed in front of you is already a huge step. I don't know, I don't know anymore, if I can go any further. You're rushing things.

Before I came here, I never thought I'd have to talk to him so much. I'm ready to offer him my body to do with as he pleases while I close my eyes to make the hour go by, but I don't want to be such an actress. Dead bitch for an hour, yes, but not an actress.

My reaction was sincere, and his gaze softens after a few seconds. But in the depths of his pupil, I can see he's not going to give up. Bingo.

- Look, I understand, but don't be afraid, trust me, everything's going to be fine. All you have to do is leave this room for a few moments and knock on this door…

I comply as quickly as possible; once again, the sooner I comply, the sooner I'll see the color of the money. My money. I've already made it mine, otherwise I don't feel able to go on.

So I make my way naked to the door and exit, not without a quick glance around to inspect the premises. What a ridiculous situation! Not to mention humiliating! If Manu or my parents could see me now… I let barely more than a second elapse before knocking. So I don't give myself any time to think about what the hell I'm doing in this damned corridor. I rush into the room. He won't make me do it again.

I stand in front of the bed, where he's still sitting.

- Now caress yourself for me. Caress yourself as if you were discovering your body for the first time.

Having learned my lesson, my hands move from my neck to my face. Without flinching, I run my fingers up the back of my neck, slowly lifting my hair, my eyes closed, as if trying to make him believe that I really appreciate what I'm doing.

I open them at one point, just to see how excited Joe is, and from there, prepare myself for a possible sudden attack of hands on me. I'm way off the mark. He's looking at me like he's watching a porn movie. His eyes are empty, expressionless. I continue my little game, letting my hands slide over the top of my breasts in the most banal gesture. I glance at my watch, which I've kept on my wrist. 14 h 29. Half an hour to go.

This context is so unrealistic for me. I don't fit into the teaser girl persona, money or no money. I'm too whole to pretend. I want to go home, what am I doing here? I can't bring myself to lower my hands any further, they get stuck in my lower abdomen. I'm not that much of an actress.

- Touch yourself more, you have to keep turning me on.

Obviously, this doesn't suit him. I lose my nerve again, dropping my arms to my sides in despondency. I don't know what to do, where to put my hands. I feel like a fool in front of him, and at the same time, I don't think I give a damn at this very moment. 14 h 34.

- I can't do it. I just can't do it.

- I see. You're more the type to be dominated… he replies in an absurdly naughty voice.

Nervously, I want to laugh again at this lame attempt at excitement, but I restrain myself. If you think about it, it's not wrong: who wants to dominate someone they don't want to? Or even to participate? Well, only one category of people: those who need money.

Only one answer would have suited him, dropped in a childish voice: "Yes, I really want you to be my master." Of course, I couldn't possibly. This isn't going at all as I'd planned. I thought I'd be fucked in no time. Just my luck to run into a pervert…

- Come on, sit down on the bed," he says after a minute of lip-smacking, "I'll take it from here.

The tone is firm and the serious business begins. Her fantasies take precedence over her personality.

After responding to his orders, I find myself sitting next to him on the dingy bedspread, which has certainly been there since the hotel opened, judging by its indefinable color, torn between blue and green.

Once again, I meet his expectations without flinching; one last effort, Laura. 2:36pm. I'm now topless on the bed. Her eyes, her face, her sex are begging for more. *Go ahead, check them out, don't be shy.* If he keeps admiring them like this, I might not even have to give him the rest of my body.

- Lie on your back.

Ouch. Smart guy. 2:41pm.

So he puts his hand on the back of my neck and gently pushes me down. It's the first time I've felt his palm on my body, the first time he's touched me.

On my back, I admire the flaking ceiling on all sides, waiting to feel his skin against mine. His hand came just as my attention slackened, and I twitched limply, not entirely surprised. First, he starts with my belly and moves slowly up to my neck. No doubt he wants to create a sensual embrace, but it can't have the slightest effect on me. His second hand comes too. The back-and-forth over my upper torso becomes rougher, more intense; he quickens the pace as his erection grows. I haven't opened my eyes once yet, trying to believe that all this is just a very bad dream.

I don't know if I want to vomit or cry from feeling his old palms on me. I'm a dead body lying on the bed. After all, he ordered a body, he's got it. If he'd asked me to do more at that moment, I'd have slapped him.

Instead, the body dance stops. He straightens up. I'm expecting another bizarre request.

- Sit down and we'll talk," he says.

I don't know if this is a joke or not. Is having to argue with him in the contract? I guess, since he's paying me, he can pretty much get away with anything.

- Why are you here today?

The ten-thousand-dollar question, or how to get a student into the swing of things.

- Do you have someone in your life? What are you doing in V.?

The questions become very personal. I'm not likely to agree to give him the real version of my life: it would be going beyond all tolerable limits to leave him a few clues about the life I lead. Besides, I'm not paid to tell the truth.

- No, I don't have anyone in my life.

14 h 49. Ten short minutes that are proving to be formidable.

- Is this money for you?

I nod. After a pause, he says:

- It's good what you're doing.

Really?

- You know, I have people who count on me too. I'm divorced, I have a daughter. A little older than you. I remarried, to a very beautiful woman, a little while ago now. Sex with her isn't really that. In fact, I gave up trying to share my fantasies with her a long time ago. It's not easy, you know, having to deal with someone who doesn't want you anymore.

What's not easy for me, at this particular moment, is to hear him unpack his life. I don't understand why he's decided to confide in me, whom he's seeing for the first time. Inevitably, if I keep listening to him, I'll start imagining his life, pasting images onto what he's like outside this room. V. is a small town, and the possibility of running into Joe on a family outing is not out of the question.

To think that when he gets out of here, he's bound to join her. I get chills all over my body. I feel sorry for his wife, wondering what she'd think if she knew that her husband regularly banged young girls and, on top of that, talked to them about her during the sessions.

- I don't want to know your life.

I'm boiling with irritation. Who does he think he is, taking advantage of others, when he's not very clear in his head and his way of thinking? I can't get a sound out of my mouth. I thought I could be a mechanical whore, and now I'm getting head lice.

Joe replies softly:

- Reassure me, you're combining business with pleasure?

The height of absurdity has now been reached. I search his eyes, his tone of voice, for some clue that he doesn't mean a word of what he's just said. He doesn't. He really thinks I'm doing all this, not just for the money, but because deep down, I really like it. In his crazy head, a woman can't give herself up just for the money, she needs another reason. And still in his crazy head, he certainly likes to think he's not that ugly. Would it be so hard for an old man whose wife no longer wants him to admit to himself that my only motivation is financial?

So I remain silent; I don't even have anger inside me anymore, I'm baffled. He then resumes the dance on my body with his hands, always touching my upper chest, breasts and belly. His skin burns me, disturbs me, but I don't let anything show. He doesn't descend to the bottom of my anatomy, my sex is still untouched by his hands, which relieves me of my despair.

- Next time, I'll bring you something, you'll see, you'll like it…

So Joe is already planning to see me again. I'm not going to yell at him that it's out of the question.

- It's okay, you can get dressed, it's time.

Liberation, it's 3pm! The end has come. Very punctual, he gets up.

He rummages in his briefcase while I hurriedly get dressed. He continues his flattery.

- I'm really happy, you know. The first contact was great, it made me really happy. You're beautiful, I wasn't expecting someone like you. What's more, you're sensitive and approachable, which I really appreciate. Of course, you were a bit reluctant at first, but I'm shy too, so it'll go better next time, you'll see.

An envelope is held out to me, and in front of him, without even asking myself whether custom or good manners oblige me to wait until I'm outside to recount, I admire my booty. It's not 100 euros, as I thought, but 250 euros that Joe hands me! Two 100-euro bills and a 50-euro bill. I've never seen a 100-euro bill. My only concern at the sight of all this money is how I'm going to get 100 euros out of my pocket without arousing suspicion. I never spend that much: 5-euro bills are more representative of my daily life.

- I'll see you on the Internet. On the other hand, if you see me on Msn, don't come and talk to me, it's often my wife who's logged on under my name.

With that, we descend in the same elevator by which we arrived. The gendarmes are no longer at reception, but at this point, I don't really care. I'm floating, this newfound money has given me wings. I'm going to be okay now, in an hour I've earned enough to get rid of a few bills that have been chasing me.

No less than 250 euros to look at me, I really took him for a ride! What a jerk, and to think he thinks we'll ever see each other again! Never, it's over, once and no more. I'm afraid he'll realize he's been tricked, so I'll hurry just in case. I also want to put the hotel out of my mind and forget it quickly.

I feel so relieved that it's all over that I can't think of anything else. I don't yet realize that Clever Joe has manipulated me with his flattery and sweet words, and that he knows exactly what he's doing.

All I can think about is this money, which is now mine and which will give me some financial breathing space for a while. I'll find another way next time. Patting my jeans pocket where the life-saving envelope lay, I smiled. Yes, once alone, I smiled victoriously.

Chapter 9

The Lover

December 12, 2006

Right after the meeting with Joe, I don't feel like going to work right away. I've got half an hour to spare. A phone call to my friends and I'm on my way to my favorite café, the one run by my buddy Paul downtown.

Arriving at the meeting place, I naturally smile. There's nothing on my face to suggest what I did half an hour ago. We exchange pleasantries, just what I need to take my mind off the previous hour. After a good hour spent checking the latest gossip, it's time to settle the bill.

- Girls, I'm sorry, but I don't have the money to pay for my coffee. Do you think you could lend it to me? I'll pay you back soon, I promise.

I can't very well take out my 100-euro bill, or even my 50-euro bill. They wouldn't understand, me never having a penny. They know me well and know that I don't often have enough to pay. They grabbed the receipt without saying a word, so that the two of them could split the bill.

- No problem, Laura. Next time, it'll be your round," laughs one of them.

She probably doesn't believe it. Most of the time, I'm so broke I can't even afford my own coffee. I often ask them to drop by my place, preferably at a bistro, so I don't have to beg. Yet when I get paid, I invite them all over for a drink, just one, but one that makes us financially comfortable.

Do they suspect anything today? I try to be myself as much as possible: happy and available. Lately it's been hard, but I've never admitted anything to them. When they come to my house, they ask me if I have any snacks, and I joke that I don't have time to go shopping.

Despite all the trouble I've taken to hide my precarious situation from them, my friends aren't fooled. Although they don't realize the importance of it, they do see that I'm struggling. They've been paying for my coffees for a long time now, so they don't really care anymore. These situations still put me in a state of temporary embarrassment. But this time, I remember having a very heavy feeling, full of guilt: the money is in my pocket. I've got enough to pay for a lot of tours with what I've just earned.

In the evening, I meet Manu in a bar, without ordering anything for me. I watch him finish his pint of beer:
- How are you, beautiful? How was your day?
- Just an ordinary day, nothing special.
You bet! It's been anything but a normal day, but I can't imagine myself telling him: "Listen, I'm fine, it's been a pretty normal day. Before work, I got groped by an old guy

I didn't know yesterday, and on top of that, he paid me 250 euros. All so I can give you the money for your rent and bills while you smoke and give rounds to everyone! Not bad, admit it."

Once his blood-alcohol level seems acceptable, we set off for our "cosy nest". He makes me laugh on the way home, telling me silly stories. Manu's always happiest when he's a bit tipsy, and I think deep down I prefer him that way.

We returned to the apartment in silence, the euphoria of the evening, of our relationship, gone. We got ready for bed like a couple who've been married for twenty years. Given the state he was in when we left the bar, maybe I can try to turn him on a little tonight. I admit I thought about it, just for a second.

Manu and I don't have much sex: he has what are commonly called "breakdowns". All couples who have been together for a few years force themselves to think that this will only be temporary. In my case, I'm beginning to find time long and personal pleasures rather tiresome. For some time now, if he doesn't come looking for me, I give up. As someone who can be defined by the gallant term "charmer", I no longer desire him. Worried, I even consulted my gynecologist, who reassured me that this kind of thing often happens when you don't feel desired by the other person. Right on the money! Between her semi-erections and my vaginal dryness, we make a great team. Like most people, I love sex and consider it essential in a couple, so it's no coincidence that my relationship with him is in serious trouble. I've reached the point where I just want him to fuck me. Before tonight. Because tonight I realized that I'll never want him again.

Strangely enough, he doesn't seem to care that much. His only interests in recent months seem to be limited to going out and taking classes. Without admitting it to ourselves, we know that our relationship is on its last legs. We accept it, without flinching, because we know there's nothing we can do about it. When love is gone, it's very difficult to catch up, even with constant effort.

So that evening, as I watched us silently brushing our teeth in front of the mirror, I realized once again that the situation couldn't go on. Our relationship is a huge farce. Is it because of what happened this afternoon? Certainly it had a triggering effect, but the tension between us has been latent for some time.

Will he talk to me, tell me anything? I feel deep down that if he doesn't say anything, if he doesn't guess what I've been through today, I won't admit it. That would mean he definitely doesn't understand me like he used to, when he knew in a second if something was wrong with me. I need his shoulders, his arms to protect me and make me forget, just tonight.

I slip between the sheets. The silence is so heavy. Not tonight, Manu, tonight I beg you, don't ignore me and take me in your arms. He joins me in bed without looking at me. Already he seems to want to adopt the position we've become accustomed to for some time now: our backs to each other. I see in his face what I've been refusing to see for months: our relationship is dead.

Now that he's lying down, and even though he's already closed his eyes, I'm still hopeful that he'll start talking. I jump in:

- Good night.
- Mhh," he replies in a sleepy voice.

Yes, good night, Manu. Bye, Manu.

Chapter 10

Loneliness

December 13, 2006

The shrill ringing of the alarm clock rouses me from my deep sleep. I couldn't fall asleep last night, tossing and turning in my bed, thinking about the day I'd had. I got up, smoked a million cigarettes in the kitchen. I even tried to work on my Italian civilization course, to no avail. My mind was too busy. It was only around 5 a.m. that, under the effect of immense fatigue, my eyes closed on their own.

Manu is still asleep. I watch his naked back turned towards me in silence. I turn off the alarm and suddenly remember. Yesterday. The nightmare. The nightmares.

Since that night, I've known that it's all over with Manu. Our relationship, which had been a model of passion and complicity in the beginning, has slowly gone up in smoke, without me being able to do anything about it. I wake up this morning feeling alone, alone in the face of my mind-numbing daily routine. I'll always remember December 12, 2006, when so much changed in my life.

But already I don't have time to think. I have to get up and go to class. All I want to do is crawl into bed and cry. But that's impossible. I know that now. I'm going to have to keep getting up every day. I'm going to have to keep living with the weight of this day. Right now, I hate myself. Even in my pyjamas, hidden by lots of fabric, it feels like my soiled body is on display for all to see. I feel as if it's oozing vice, as if you can't help looking at it because it radiates such ugliness. I feel horribly dirty. Would it be worse if Joe had possessed me completely?

I stagger to my feet. My body feels impossible to carry. In the bathroom, I let the water run over my body for a quarter of an hour, at first without moving. Then I grab a sponge and rub it over my skin with all my might. Suddenly, my skin turns red from the intense scratching. I don't care, I can't stop. I'd like to wash away all this dirt and pretend yesterday never happened. I lost everything yesterday: Manu and my self-esteem. For 250 euros.

I run to catch the metro. I'm caught up in reality: I don't even have time to lament my fate, I have to leave to study. But how can this be? I know I won't be able to concentrate, listen or read anything. There are voices in my head that keep telling me I'm nothing but a whore. I sold my body for money. I gave myself to a stranger for money while my boyfriend was at school. I'm worthless, I'm dirty and I have a feeling I'll stay that way for the rest of my life.

I dress in silence and slowly close the apartment door on my relationship with Manu. I'll never be able to look at him with the same innocence again. I didn't just deceive him, it goes beyond that. I've deceived myself, I've prostituted myself. The word tears at my throat when I say it. But it comes back naturally, because that's what happened.

It's freezing this morning. I'm walking fast, to outrun the icy wind, and who knows, maybe this pace will anaesthetize my thoughts. I feel discouraged, ashamed, I don't even have the strength to cry.

The journey to college didn't help matters. When you're sitting on the subway, you start to think, to reflect. Even if you don't want to, you're forced to think about yourself, your life, who you are. I think, without realizing it, without wanting to. I feel like everyone can read on my face what I did yesterday. I feel myself blushing, and I bury my face in the big scarf around my neck.

Even if I stayed with Manu, I'm sure he'd understand sooner or later what I'd done. My sin is too present in my head not to be seen from the outside. I'm tired from my short night, but today I know I won't even be able to doze off. Struggling wasn't enough, now I'll have to pay for the rest of my life with my thoughts.

I leave the metro in a state of disarray, this life review is much worse than it was before. One thing's for sure: my studies will be my refuge. Apart from that, Manu was the only thing really worth spending my energy on, the only thing worth giving of myself. Now that it's all over, I can't afford to let myself go. I've got to get on with my life. I made a mistake, but I promise myself it will never happen again. The proof is in the pudding: just once was enough to make me lose the boy I loved. Never again.

Chapter 11

The Parking Lot

December 22, 2006

"Never again!" It was to be expected after all, once the bills were paid, the rent handed over to Manu, I had nothing left. I'm in trouble again, and need to find a place to sleep. But how? A friend from college agrees to put me up for a while. She lives alone in her apartment, and I think she's quite happy to have company.

At her place, I'm getting ready for an appointment. I answered one of the countless ads again: there's no shortage of female students, so I easily found a new prey.

Life went on as usual and so did I, on my own, trying to get by. Looking for another apartment, I'm obviously faced with a lot of expenses that I can't cover on my telemarketing salary alone. Once again, I find myself in an apparent financial bind. It's no longer just a simple hassle: I feel that if I don't do something, all this will become recurrent and I'll never be able to keep my head above water. If I want to live in my own apartment, this is the price I have to pay.

I already have a job and my courses, what more can I do? I ask myself this question knowing the answer in advance. This door remains open despite all the promises I've made to myself.

The first time with Joe, which in my mind isn't really a first time because it's so far removed from anything we can imagine, awakens mixed feelings in me. Putting myself naked in front of him, having to endure his fantasies, threw me for a loop. In spite of everything, I still felt I'd pigeonholed him. In the end, it was a terrible first time, because now that I've run out of money again, I can't seem to put it out of my mind.

So I got in touch with another guy. In a trance in front of a discreet university computer, I gave in again. Still in the same frame of mind, I'm only planning this meeting to replenish the coffers, to get rid of all the expenses I still have to make for the apartment. We've worked out a rate of 70 euros an hour for two hours. Plus, of course, the restaurant, which he would pay for.

He's young, only 26, and his name is Julien. Maybe, I thought, it would be easier with him than with an old guy like Joe. I'm also curious about his motivations, what makes him willing to pay a prostitute. It seems to me that at his age, finding a girl isn't all that difficult.

We meet in front of a restaurant downtown. This time, if I meet someone, finding an explanation won't be a challenge. We're from the same generation, which helps a lot. People wouldn't wonder as much as they might have if they'd seen me with Joe.

I don't have to wait for him, he's already here when I arrive. In one look, I understand why he contacted me. He's carrying a huge amount of frustration with him. Physically, he's more than ordinary: not particularly tall, nor really short, he stands in a hunched-over way. He has a terrible hairstyle, one that instantly classifies him, once again, in the redneck category: his hair is pulled up in a sort of brush cut that goes off to the sides. No style from this point of view.

His attire leaves something to be desired too, I say to myself once more, inclined to hate. Bland burgundy wool sweater, uncut jeans and musty sneakers. The overall look was ridiculous. Typical of the kind of poor guy I'd never turn my back on in the street. On the other hand, he could well have been the target of my giggles with my girlfriends. Are we cruel? Maybe we are.

We gave each other a peck on the lips. He's visibly embarrassed and already seems to regret having come. As we enter the restaurant, I hope people don't think we're together. Misplaced pride. I'm glad I didn't overdress for the evening: just jeans and a little top, sexy but not too much.

The place is just like it: plain. No decoration, white walls, just tables lined up in order. The naked white light is probably what bothers me most, because it exposes us too much. So I can contemplate the place we're in: dreadful. The restaurateur hasn't even tried to give the impression of a guinguette à la bonne franquette, which I would have liked. So bad taste must follow me through my experience as a prostitute, reminding me a little more each time of what I do. In any case, even if I had enjoyed the place, coming here with a customer mentally prevents me from returning in the future. A customer? Yes, a customer, since I'm a whore.

The waitress seats us at a table close to another couple. The restaurant is packed and all the tables are next to each other. I can feel Julien stiffen a little; he would have preferred a more secluded table so as not to be noticed. Once seated, we remain silent for a while, and I can tell that he's rubbing his hands nervously under the table, not knowing how to start a conversation. I decide to help him a little, out of pity and above all because I refuse to spend a whole evening without conversation.

- What do you do for a living?

- I work for a company in the suburbs of V. It's a pretty interesting job and I'm…

It only took one sentence for me to get bored. Keeping my eyes fixed on him, I ignore the rest and let my thoughts wander. The next day, I won't be able to remember what he told me that night. I'll just remember a long tirade, a soporific monologue that reassured him and allowed him to hide his obvious embarrassment. This guy is really uninteresting, just like his job.

Afraid of dying of boredom, and no longer able to hide the fact that I'm as bored as a dead rat, I start to provoke him a little. It's one of my biggest faults in life: as soon as I spot a weakness in someone, cruelly, I take advantage of it. I have a lot of self-doubt myself, but I always manage not to let it show. So it's hard for me to understand people who can't do it. Clearly, this guy's a loser, I tell myself, and, unluckily for him, it shows in his behavior.

I cut him off dead in his mind-numbing speech, without any embarrassment:

- Why did you come here today?

- Here? You mean, why did I choose this restaurant?

- Of course not! Here, with me. Why did you post an ad looking for a "masseuse"?

I obviously threw him off balance. My affront and provocative tone make him uncomfortable. He looks frantically to his right and left to see if anyone has heard my remark. I can already see the beads of sweat on his forehead. What a jerk! Does he really think I'm going to spend the whole meal pretending to ignore the fact that all he wants to do is fuck me? Unless deep down he doesn't really know what he wants.

- Well… er… it's quite complicated, you know… I've never done this sort of thing before, it's the first time.

Spit it out that you're horny. In my head, I'm becoming very vulgar.

- Well, I'm married… to someone very nice, perfect in fact… but when it comes to sex… I don't really know what's going on… it's complicated…

- I'm sure it's not that complicated. Your wife's frigid, isn't she?

I didn't mince my words there. He straightens in surprise, then lets his shoulders drop, as if to approve what I've just said. This guy's got taboos I've broken in a second. Shit, there's no reason I should be the only one to suffer.

- Let's just say she doesn't really want me. At first, I thought it would go away, that it wouldn't last, you know? We've been married for a year now, but nothing's changed sexually speaking, on the contrary. She pushes me away all the time and I don't dare force her or talk about it with her. I don't have many friends to talk to about it either and…

The Parking Lot

It was clear now, this guy was desperate. Certainly married too soon to his childhood sweetheart, no mates to party with, he turns to prostitutes to drown his sorrows. He has no real social life and hopes to fill the void with me tonight. Once again, he launches into an endless soliloquy, explaining that he's very lonely, that his job doesn't interest him in the least, and many other things that I forget as soon as he says them. Again, I cut him off abruptly:

- A couple without sex is just a friendship," I say curtly.

He looks at me as if I've just said something terrible. I only half mean what I've just said, but this guy exasperates me, and in his presence I feel in a cruel mood. However, he remains downcast at my affront.

I realize, at this very moment, that the life of a fille de joie doesn't stop at sex. Customers often contact prostitutes just to talk, to relieve themselves of their boring or hindered lives. I'm not prepared to put up with this, to listen to the horny man complain. I have my own problems and, even if there is no scale of pain, it's more than I can bear. The conversation takes a dangerous turn, and now veers into something far too personal for my liking. I'm becoming his shrink-ass. This guy is forcing me to think, and that shouldn't be compatible with the Laura fille de joie. It's not exactly joyful.

As the meal progresses, I learn more and more about his life and literally sink into his daily routine. The worst thing is that, in other circumstances, I would certainly have found this guy very endearing. In another context, I'd probably have consoled him, but now I'm incapable of doing so. Tired of hearing him complain, I cut him off:

- Well, say it, are you horny?

He twitches. I scare him and myself. So much vulgarity and provocation! But I can't help it. I'm bored of this guy beating around the bush, so I've decided to take matters into my own hands and put an end to this evening.

- Uh… yes," he finally lets out in a breath, relieved to have been exorcised at last.

- Well then, it's time to go, isn't it?

I see him panic.

- Uh… go? You mean now?

- Yes, now we've talked enough for tonight.

I can't take this endless discussion anymore. This guy contacted me to get a "massage", and instead we end up in this dingy restaurant discussing his empty existence. I want to put an end to this charade as soon as possible.

- But where? In a hotel?

- Do you have money for a hotel?

- You know, I don't know… I don't know if I really want to anymore.

- Of course you do. If you've contacted me, it's because you want to.

He plunges his puppy-dog gaze into mine for a few seconds. I've wounded his ego, and however low he may be right now, he's having a hard time accepting it. The last thing on my mind is to go home without my money after an evening like that. After a few minutes, he lets out in a breath, as if not to have to repeat it:

- I know a parking lot near here…

Without a second thought, he settled the bill. He let me into his car and, without a word, we headed for the famous

The Parking Lot

supermarket parking lot. The night is very dark, and it's hard to see anything. I feel protected this way, no one will see us.

For all the aplomb he's armed himself with as he leaves the restaurant, I once again sense that Julien is very uncomfortable when he has to turn off the ignition. He's still rubbing his hands together nervously, trying to distract us by fiddling with the buttons on his car. He's afraid someone will find us here, and I have to admit I have the same fears as he does.

- Are you cold?

It's the middle of winter, and the cool of the night is catching up with us. It's a creepy situation: the two of us, in a car in this parking lot, making sure no one sees us having sex.

- Yes, a little.

- All right, I'll put the heating on.

I light a cigarette without asking permission. He turns on the heater, and as the warmth fills the car, he continues to rub his hands. In the face of his indecision, I decide to take the plunge. I put my hand on his jeans, at crotch level. He has no erection. I look up at him, searching for an explanation I already know. Without breaking eye contact, he says:

- I'm uh… pretty stressed…

To stop him talking again, I start rubbing his jeans harder. No reaction. For a good five minutes, I continue my task. I'm convinced that if he doesn't get what he wants, he'll end the date and won't pay me. Having endured the whole evening psychologically, I can't leave without a reward. Embarrassed at having no physical reply, he stammers shyly:

- Maybe if you got naked…

First approach! I'm surprised by this unexpected repartee: it doesn't at all match his tone of voice, his way of being. I undress all the same, in this car lost in the middle of the parking lot. At this moment, I'm only dreading one thing: that someone will discover us. Clearly, Julien shares the same fear as I do.

After a few minutes of observing my naked body, he allows himself to touch it. I rest my hand on his jeans, to no avail. He touches my breasts first, kneading them carefully. He clearly doesn't dare go any lower, preferring to concentrate on my torso. He doesn't seem to react to my back-and-forth on his pants. After a few minutes, desperate to see the nothingness of the situation, he announces:

- Say, would you like to…

I immediately understand what he wants. You don't need a 5-year degree in prostitution for that.

I unbutton his pants and start giving him oral sex. Little by little I can feel the excitement building up inside him. In no time at all, he takes off his jeans and tips over the passenger seat. He puts his body on mine for a moment, takes out his condom, then a few seconds later comes inside me.

I can't explain what I'm feeling right now. Disgust, certainly. My head is elsewhere, I can't feel anything. Julien has become a "he", an impersonal "he". The first "he". It's too much, I can't stand it inside me, I don't want it inside me. Everything becomes a blur, I close my eyes. I already feel so dirty. I grit my teeth in disgust. I feel an immense emptiness. In my head, I keep repeating to myself: "That's it, you're a prostitute, you're surrendering your entire body to a stranger's sex."

I'm not a smarty-pants anymore. No more provocation, no more showing off. In the end, he wins; he gets what he wants. I have to think of the money, not forget my goal, but the moment is too hard. I've never felt so far from myself. I have no more tears to cry, only nausea to express my mal de vivre, bills piling up to force me to understand why I'm doing this. Manu, where are you? How did I get here? I don't want him to touch me anymore, why do I have to put up with this? The injustice of my situation makes me grit my teeth to keep from screaming. "It'll soon be over, Laura, don't open your eyes, it'll soon be over."

It must be said that he quickly stopped. He came and his conscience is now taking over from his libido:

- Uh… Laura… we'd better go.

I don't look at him. I almost weep with joy at the knowledge that all this won't last.

- I'll pay you for the two hours, don't worry. I'll give you 140 euros.

- Yes, all right.

The money smells like the one Joe gave me: it's fast and taboo. Absolutely not easy.

- I'll take you home, okay?

I nod. We set off in silence. I can't utter a word.

Long before we reach my house, I ask him to stop. We kiss quickly, both feeling rather awkward.

- Goodbye.

- Goodbye, Laura. All the best.

I get out of the car without asking for help. It starts right up.

Yes, I'll need courage. To accept not only the stain, but also the idea that I'm already addicted to this money that's so quickly falling into my hands.

I hurry home through the dark, icy night. While Julien is already driving towards his wife, who is waiting for him in the warmth, I fall asleep alone in my bed. I'm so cold.

Chapter 12

The Look

December 24, 2006

On the table set by my mother for the occasion are a multitude of dishes, each more appetizing than the last. And as usual for the past three months, I'm as hungry as a wolf. There are five of us at the table tonight. My father has brought along a friend of his so he won't have to spend Christmas alone. I'm always moved when I see my father do things like this, but I can't understand why he doesn't do the same with me.

The presence of this friend livens up the evening and everyone chats happily. Everyone but me. I don't feel like celebrating, I can't do it. These supposed Christmas vacations are in fact a poisoned chalice for me. Back-to-school exams force me to study harder. I continue to work, underpaid, at the telemarketing company during the two-week vacation; I can't afford to take days off. I have to earn money. But when I'm not working, I'm just going around in circles at home. The fact that I haven't been going to university for the last few days has destabilized me. Studies are my refuge from thinking. Going to university allows me to get away from home, to have a minimum of social life. I've hardly seen any of my friends since September. My schedule is divided between university and telemarketing. The rest of my free time is entirely devoted to my studies, my reading and my courses.

This family reunion is a masquerade. My father plays the perfect guest, ostentatiously re-serving his friend. He's even pampering me, wanting to project the image of a perfect, caring father. I listen to my father talk, as he never does when it's just the four of us. My father is a magician, he knows how to transform himself in public and put on a mask.

It doesn't work with me. In other years, I would have accepted this little game, even knowing that the next day he wouldn't speak to me. I would have taken the opportunity to give him a hug. I would have agreed to pretend that we're very close, simply because I'm dying to. But this year is different. I'm tired of begging for his love, I can't stand being ignored like this. If he really cared, he'd have realized a long time ago that I'm struggling like nobody's business, that I've lost over twelve kilos since September, that I'm working myself to the bone, that I suffer to the point of tears every day. Maybe if he took the time to look at me as a person, he'd understand what I have to do to find money.

I ask myself too many questions to enjoy the evening. I ruin my father's plan: the guest can see I'm not in the mood to brag. I don't care about my father's disapproving looks, I don't want to act anymore. My mother tries to fill the silences as best she can. She's probably afraid I'll say something insolent or derogatory. My father relies on my sister to make conversation. He asks her an avalanche of questions about high school, her friends, so many that she hardly has time to catch her breath. But she's delighted by the situation: she feels like she's really being listened to for once.

After an incredibly hearty dinner, it's time to open presents. My mother loves Christmas and is very careful to respect tradition. She set up a big tree in the living room, and put the presents at the foot of it. As she does every year, she has also brought out the whole nativity scene. No one in my family is religious, not even her, but she loves to play along. I know that deep down she regrets not being able to give us a fantastic Christmas with thousands of presents. So, as if to make up for it, she goes all out on the decorations. I adore my mother and I'm moved by all the trouble she goes to to make sure we're happy, not just at Christmas, but all year round. She's a full-time mother hen, even though she's always talked to us like adults. And she succeeds: to see this crib filled with little characters and the tree glittering, I'm happy to be with her tonight.

No mountain of presents for us at Christmas, we've always been used to getting just one. Mom always manages to find us something of particular importance, to make us forget that we're only getting one. My sister and I don't really care about all that anymore, even though when we were little we used to be crazy with jealousy when our school friends showed off gifts straight out of a thousand and one nights. Over time, I've come to think of it as a normal reaction.

This year, more than last, I'm not expecting anything special. I haven't asked for anything in particular, so much so that I feel I need everything. But "everything" is unattainable, utopian for my parents.

So I open the gift intended for me. I tear open the apple-green paper slowly and discover a pair of black heels. I'd seen them with my mother in a store on All Saints' Day, and told her I liked them. I wouldn't have thought she'd gone back to buy them afterwards. I give my mother a big hug to thank her. Even though I know he had nothing to do with the choice of gift, I thank my father from afar. We don't hug or kiss.

I think of Manu. I haven't heard from him since we split up. My parents were relieved that we weren't living together anymore, they never really liked him, finding him a snob. I don't think anyone will ever be good enough for me and my sister in my mother's eyes.

If she'd known… She would certainly have hated Manu even more. First, she would have cried for days on end. Then her sadness would turn to anger and she'd look for someone to blame. First she would have blamed herself, then Manu. When she found out how much he was charging me, with hardly any outlay, she would have held him responsible for my prostitution. She would have gone into a rage. She would have tried to find answers, but without success. In time, all this would have been a bad memory, and she would have helped me forget it. But she would have spent the rest of her life with this wound, blaming herself forever. No, she must never know.

The evening passes quietly, without any outbursts or arguments. I decide to go to my room quite early. I want to get up early tomorrow to study. In the afternoon, I'll be back on the train, as I'll be working at the telemarketing company from December 26. No time to breathe, but it'll pay off one day, it's bound to.

I quickly head off to bed, with a general wave to the assembly. Once in my room, I work on a Spanish text. I can't help it, as soon as I find a minute, I revise. I know I'm going to pass my exams with no problem, I've worked far too hard for that. But I can't help it, I'm a perfectionist, everything has to be perfect. Besides, working prevents me from thinking about anything else.

The very next day, I'm on a train back to V. And as usual, I don't have much to say about the two days I spent with my parents.

Chapter 13

Oppression

January 7, 2007

Unfortunately, my experience with Julien didn't stop me. It had the exact opposite effect. The new ads on the Internet never stop, and it sometimes seems to me that the world is full of dissatisfied people who will never be satisfied. I don't spit on it though, since these strangers and their wild desires temporarily help me solve my financial problems.

So I make contact with an older man, almost certainly for fear of running into a penniless indecisive like Julien. This time, the guy's name is Pierre. All I know about his life is his profession: businessman in a well-known company. This made me feel confident, as it implied a really reassuring financial situation. The decision is hard enough, and this business is like Russian roulette. I might as well be sure, as far as possible, of getting paid. A rendezvous has been set for early afternoon in the town's main square. He prefers us to meet downtown and then leave for his place, where, he says, "we'll be quieter". At first, I refused: there was no way I was

"

going to end up in the home of someone I didn't know, where anything could happen to me. But after some thought, he managed to convince me: we'd be safe from anyone's possible gaze, since his apartment is empty. He, too, values his anonymity and doesn't want to risk being spotted in a city hotel where he might meet people. So our last e-mail concluded with him discreetly picking me up and taking me to his place in his car. I figure I'll know if I can trust him when I see him after all. I realize the danger I'm exposing myself to by doing this, but I need the money. I always want more now.

At the appointed hour, I walk towards the famous square in the center of V. I've put on one of my favorite dresses: gray, puffy at the shoulders. It accentuates my waist and shows off a bit of my legs, which I've tucked into a pair of fashionable boots. I look very elegant in this outfit, and I know the effect it has on men. It gives me a childlike air that draws the eye. I've clearly put it on for financial reasons: the better I look, the more he'll be willing to pay. Besides, today is a beautiful, sunny winter's day. I woke up in a good mood and just wanted to look pretty. For me, not for him. As I drive along, I can already see the men staring at me and admiring my dress without a word. Yes, today I know I'm pretty.

In the distance, I can see lively stalls and crowds gathered around the victuals on display. I'd forgotten! Today, there's a fair on the main square where producers sell their local produce to curious tourists. This in itself is both a good and a bad thing: with so many people, I can easily get lost in the crowd. However, I also run the risk of bumping into people I know, and this feeling quickly turns into immense fear.

I decided to stand back a little from all the commotion, so that I could quickly spot the man called Pierre and drag him along. He tells me he'll be wearing a black suit with a red scarf, something that's not only noticeable but also weather-appropriate.

Watching the passers-by, I start to get impatient after five minutes. I'm uncomfortable and clap my hands nervously on my crossed arms. I'm convinced that the people around me are noticing my odd attitude, which makes me all the more paranoid.

Suddenly, I hear someone shouting my name behind me, someone with a voice more than familiar. I recognize it immediately, and it makes my blood run cold.

- Laura! Laura! Laura! Laura!

I admit I thought about not turning around, cowardly, and running away. Instead, I turn my head in a slow, natural movement.

- Mommy? Mommy? What are you doing here?

I stammered, trying to control my inner panic.

My mother. Here, in the town square. While I wait for a customer to pay me to let him possess me. I'm petrified, like a child who's just been caught with her fingers full of jam before dinner. I stammer, knowing that if I don't speak intelligibly right away, my mother will suspect something is wrong.

- Did you know that the whole family from Nantes was visiting us today? Remember them? We thought it would be fun to come and have a look around here together, to show them a bit of V.

Ah yes, very nice indeed. Behind her are my father and the famous representatives of what she called "the family".

Oppression

I completely forgot about that factor: the fair, my family being there this weekend, my parents potentially able to come to the fucking fair. Nice picture: my mother, my father, my aunt and uncle and two or three other strangers I haven't seen more than three times in my life, but who I recognize as part of my genealogy. I'm stuck, I have to make an excuse immediately. I try not to look around for the unknown Pierre, but I can't help casting furtive glances left and right.

My mother must sense that I'm not really listening to her, but she can't imagine why. Enthused by this unexpected reunion, she decides to express her joy to our family behind her. I'm afraid that if someone shouts my name too loudly, a suit in a red scarf will turn around and address me.

- Hey, look who's here! It's Laura!

- Ah, but it's Laura! What a pleasant surprise! How you've changed! A real woman! Were you coming to meet us? my aunt enthused.

I love my aunt very much, even though I see her very little, but today I couldn't give a damn. I find myself in the middle of a huge family reunion in the town square, while I, the prostitute, am waiting for one of my clients. What an idea, too, to make an appointment here in the middle of the afternoon! I've been stupid, but it's too late to complain now, we've got to get out of this situation as soon as possible.

Suddenly, I spot a red scarf fluttering in the wind. The man wearing it has his back to me and is walking towards the center of the square. He, too, must have been waiting for me on the side and, not seeing me coming, tries to make sure he hasn't been taken in. He's in his fifties, wears a suit and looks very elegant. I know in a second that this is my man.

I'm interrupted in my stupor by my aunt, who is still waiting for an answer.

- So Laura, are you dreaming?

She and my mother turn to see what I'm staring at so intently. Fortunately, Pierre the businessman has disappeared into the crowd.

- Uh… yes, sorry, a little bit," I say, smiling to cut short their enquiring glances. I've been waiting for some friends for a while now, I thought I'd seen them, but I was wrong.

Suddenly I'm dragging my mother and aunt by the arm away from where the man is standing. As if we were three good girlfriends. I see my father and the rest of the family following us, chatting away.

- Ah, of course, the little girl's busy - it's normal at her age! We won't bother you any longer, pretty Laura; let's get back to our shopping! Do you know how beautiful this city is?

She can't stop talking. My aunt is a real chatterbox. My old businessman had to run off. The prospect of losing money because of an unwelcome encounter with my family haunts me. Even though two worlds that don't mix have brushed up against each other today, I need this money to keep my head above water. I'm aware that I'm playing with fire, but inside me, a voice keeps telling me that I can't do otherwise.

Unable to stop myself, my eyes resume their mad back and forth over the sides. My aunt doesn't notice, but my mother does.

- Come on, let's get back on the road, have a good afternoon with your girlfriends, darling. Come to the house for dinner

Oppression

tonight, if you like. We can pick you up after our errands, you spend the evening with us, and then you're on the train home tomorrow. I know it's a bit long but... Or maybe you've got something planned...

- I'll see, Mom, that's nice. I don't know what I'm going to do yet. I have to work tomorrow, you know...

In fact, I'm already working. I bid a seemingly endless farewell to my family. My aunt gives me a long hug, murmuring that she hopes to see me tonight, that I'm very pretty and blah, blah, blah... My father, on the other hand, waves at me, paying me no real attention. Does he sense vice and sin on my skin?

I'm off, hopping along like nothing, but in my head, I'm running at full speed. I try to look around discreetly so I can spot my man; I know my mother is still watching me. I keep my fingers crossed that he hasn't run off in the face of my blatant tardiness.

Looking around for a scarf, I suddenly spot him at the other end of the square. I've done such a good job of dragging my family away from him that now he's on the opposite side of the square from me, I have to be discreet again. I'm determined to get that money today. The meeting with my parents was a cold shower, but I have no time to think about it, no time to reflect.

I finally reach my businessman, slowing my pace so as not to attract attention. The man isn't expecting anyone in particular, I haven't described myself, and at this moment, I don't regret it. He paces in front of me. I stick right behind him and push past. Once I'm level with him, I whisper to him in true drug-dealer fashion:

- It's me Laura, follow me. Don't turn around and keep moving, my family's here.

I said this sentence in a breath. I can feel the pressure all around me, and I want to escape this oppressive situation as quickly as possible.

I can feel him walking behind me, dutifully following my pace. I continue my track-and-field walk for a good five minutes without looking back once. When I'm sure we're out of harm's way, I stop to catch my breath on a deserted street.

I can see him from the front. He's quite tall and not bad-looking. With his suit on, you can tell he's trying to do an imitation of James Bond on the comeback trail. Rather successful in terms of class, less so for speed of execution. I'd say he's well into his fifties, given a closer look at his body. However, he definitely looks his best in the suit. But the second I set eyes on his face, I'm disappointed. His eyes are a very pale blue, which in itself is quite bewitching, but they're empty of any energy. This guy looks like he's lived an exhausting ten years, and now he's got nothing left.

Between him disguised as a gracious businessman and me as a sexy young student, we make a fine couple: a father with his daughter, whom he would have raised well and taught to dress elegantly, but certainly not a 19-year-old prostitute with her client.

- Hello, Laura. What a run!

He speaks so slowly that I can't even see the end of his short sentence.

- Hello, Pierre. Pierre, right?

- Yes, that's it. What do you say we go and sit in a bar for a few minutes to recover from our emotions? Then we'll be on our way.

A lounge bar around the corner is our refuge. Firstly, because neither he nor I want to keep running the streets, and also because I want to hide from people quickly. I've seen too much for one day. We sit down at a table in the back.

After placing my order, there's a few minutes' silence, which gives me time to examine the place. The waiters match the place: handsome, very hip. However, they stare at us strangely, whispering amongst themselves. I frown at first when, as they bring us our drinks, one of them doesn't respond to my "thank you" and smile. In a flash, I guess the reason for such coldness. The youngster has realized that we're not father and daughter, despite our clever disguises. I can imagine him snapping at me as he goes back behind the bar to make coffees for other, more decent customers: "Wait a minute, I swear! She's a whore, and he's either her pimp or her customer! It's obvious!"

Is it that obvious? Pierre doesn't seem to have noticed, and I don't dare mention it. He starts the conversation quietly.

- Shall we finish our coffees and go back to my place?

Yes, the sooner the better. Halfway through a sip of coffee, I nod in agreement. What I'm sure of after just a few minutes with him is that he's too soft to do me any harm. All the same, I'm still on my guard: as the saying goes, "sleeping dogs lie in wait".

- We'll be quieter than at the hotel, as there's no one at my place at the moment. You'll see, you'll like it, it's a beautiful place. I'm the owner…

After Julien, there's no way I'm going to let myself be fooled again. I don't want to hear anything about his life and I let him know right away. It's for reasons like these that I don't want to go to cafés with customers: they encourage a conviviality that I don't want to indulge in. I wouldn't be a good escort.

Five minutes later, we're walking outside to his car. As he plays Formula 1 driver behind the wheel of his luxury automobile, I dream of the place he's taking me to: a big, beautiful house with a big garden, in a faraway suburb where there are no neighbors around. One day, I'll have the same.

Pierre remaining silent, I have more than enough time to panic and begin to measure the consequences of my act. After all, I don't know where I'm going or what I'm going to run into. I've taken a risk this time: who knows, the gentleman who talks slower than his shadow might suddenly turn out to be a cocaine addict who, once he's had his fill, will jump all over me. Hm, seeing him like this, who takes a good ten minutes at a deserted stop to check if the road is clear, I doubt it.

When it stops after only a quarter of an hour's travel, we're standing in front of huge, luxurious buildings in a sought-after part of town. Very modern, they frame and define the heart of V. From the top, there must be a superb view. Pierre gets out of the car. His endless footsteps are aging him, despite his dynamic business suit. The walk to his apartment is as long as it is hard.

We finally reach his floor. The sumptuous corridors are clean, empty, impeccable. Everything the rich like. It was like being in a real private hotel. We're standing in front of his door, where I tell myself the ordeal of the key awaits us. I want

Oppression

to snatch it out of his hands and turn it in the lock myself. I've already had enough, and I have a feeling I'm going to find the time very long in his presence.

Fortunately, I'm distracted for a moment from this desolate spectacle when we finally enter his lair. Pierre the snail crawls upright into the kitchen, leaving me for a few moments to admire the view of his interior. The room that first catches my eye is the living room: fantastically large, white, a real rap video cliché. The sunny day makes its luxurious furnishings all the more striking: minimalist throughout, the few decorative objects adorning the shelves are African ebony statuettes. Tasteful and good in a very big package.

I'm torn between an inevitable modesty in the face of all this opulence and a strange pride that's not devoid of relief: he hasn't lied to me, he's making a good living. All that matters now is that I don't end up in an ambush surrounded by libidinous debauchers.

I don't have time to rejoice at my fate - it's all relative - when Pierre arrives in gastropod mode with a tray of glasses. He places it on the coffee table, then turns to me and says:

- Well, I thought you might like a snack before…

His sentence hangs in the air. He and I both know what's coming next. I inspect the victuals. He's brought me a glass of milk and a slice of gingerbread. Damn! This guy really takes me for a kid, he's cultivating the woman-child fantasy to the hilt. I didn't realize what a fantasy I am for the customers. Or is it just him? Because of my childish dress? Pierre sees me as a child, but a child he'd like to grope. There's something wrong with this picture. I accept the snack without a word, already grabbing the gingerbread to appease my hunger. I drink the glass of milk.

Pierre stands with one hand on his hip in a totally unnatural way. He watches me peck at the slice of cake with a smile, proud of his child who is feeding to build up his strength. I drop my gingerbread suddenly, looking up at him. I'm about to light my cigarette when Pierre says:

- On the other hand, there's no smoking at my place.

My only response is to spit out the smoke and stare into his eyes. He's confused by this and, not knowing how to react, prefers to concentrate on something else.

- A little music?" he suddenly says.

Armed with the remote control, he switched on the hi-fi system, which didn't seem ready to respond to his commands. After a few minutes' agonizing over it, he goes to have a look at the problem for himself. The height of ridiculousness: the rich businessman buys equipment for the sole reason that it's expensive, but doesn't know how to use it. His attempts to create a languorous atmosphere are pathetic. Everything he has meticulously planned falls through. I don't even smile anymore, I'm bored of this guy.

After several minutes of effort, I finally hear the music. I recognize it immediately. Luz Casal. This singer with her heavenly voice rocked my childhood and adolescence. She's my father's favorite singer. She's literally part of the family: we know all her albums, not just those for which she's recently become a household name. I've never wondered whether I like her music or not: her records are on repeat at home. She was introduced to me at an age when you don't ask questions about your parents' tastes: you like what they like because you cherish them. As a result, Luz Casal logically comes to mind when I think of home, of my family.

Pierre couldn't have made a worse choice. I have a very special relationship with this woman, an untouchable relationship that he can't appropriate. Sitting cross-legged in front of his coffee table, mouth full of gingerbread, I'm outraged that he should usurp the harmony that reigns between Luz Casal and my family. Once again today - once too often - my private life has been dangerously mixed up with my life as a prostitute. I know in my heart that Pierre has nothing to do with it and that, not knowing me, he could never have guessed. But even so, I can't help hating him now, just for making me think.

My eyes must be casting real black swords in his direction, because the businessman has been staring at me for a while, trying to pierce my thoughts.

- I hate this singer. Can you please stop the music?

Surprised that I'd suddenly come out of my silence, Pierre carries out what sounds more like an order than a request for a favor. There's silence again.

Certainly to avoid conversation, he approaches me, slowly of course. As he advances, I can feel his excitement growing. The room reeks of sex with every step he takes towards me. I don't move, I can't bring myself to touch him.

I watch him make his way towards me. When he reaches my height, his crotch is literally in front of my eyes. He holds this position for several seconds, clearly enjoying it. He unbuttons his suit pants, sliding them down his legs. This situation makes me nauseous. I know I've reached my limit today.

I make myself an inner promise not to give him anything. It's too late for him; I now hold him stupidly responsible for my sadness, for my prostitution. So far, this date hasn't gone at all well. He's got it all wrong. Even his eyelashes exasperate me with their laziness.

He finally offers me his hand to get up. Standing in front of him, I realize how tall he is: I'm right up to his mouth.

Pierre removes my dress. I'm now in my underwear in front of him, my legs slipped into cheap stockings. It doesn't matter to him, he finds me to his liking, I can tell by his panting breath. He takes me into his bedroom and gently pushes me onto his huge bed. He takes advantage of my reclining position to get rid of his shirt. Leaning towards me, he turns me over and puts me on my stomach. I let him do it to me like a blow-up doll.

- I'm going to give you a massage, do you like it?

- Hm… yes yes…

Pierre lays his whole body on top of mine. I crumble under his weight. I free myself with an upward thrust of my posterior, which startles him. Released, I resume normal breathing. He places his body alongside mine and starts to caress me. He's left my bra on, and I suspect it's because he doesn't know how to take it off. I wish I'd run away. A dilemma is brewing in my mind: maybe I should leave after all, if I don't feel it. A glance at his clock radio informs me that I have barely twenty minutes left. The lure of money drives my decision. I'm prepared to wait for this money, which I think I've earned.

His hands move over my body at the expected speed, unsurprisingly, too slowly for me not to see the passage of time. I'm completely still: if someone were to walk in right now, they might think I was dead.

For exactly eighteen minutes, he rubs himself against me without trying anything else. My silent reticence must be too threatening for him to dare. He doesn't utter a word, content with this contact. I close my eyes, it's the right thing to do. When the alarm clock, with its red light, finally displays the saving hour, I leap out of bed without a word. Pierre gets up obediently, and doesn't even sigh at my haste to get out.

Silently, I look at him to indicate that he should follow me into the living room. He plunges his paternalistic hand into his wallet, like a father who deigns to give his daughter a few bucks so she can go out and have fun with her friends. He takes out 150 euros, for two hours. Quite a haul for what was consumed - next to nothing. Even so, I'm firmly convinced that the money was hard-earned and is rightfully mine.

Although I've been sure of it ever since I met him in the square, I know I'll never see Pierre again. He's now too closely linked in my mind to a feeling of disgust. And above all, to an unwelcome encounter with my parents. Reasonably, I know that this fate could have befallen anyone, but my thoughts stubbornly associate him, make him responsible. He's the reason I went to the town square this morning, the reason I had to lie to my family (to whom, so far, I've only "failed to tell").

Pierre offers to give me a lift home, but I decline: I'm not going to spend another minute in his company. If I have to walk two days back to V., I'll do it. I pocket the money, almost snatching it out of his hands, and run out the door without asking for anything else. Leaving Pierre alone in his luxurious château, I leave without looking back, muttering an inaudible "goodbye".

- Shall we get in touch soon, Laura?

- Hm… Yes.

I don't mean a word of it. But I prefer to lie, to avoid any endless explanations, and above all, so that he doesn't get angry with me. I know my lie is protected: this guy only has my e-mail, nothing else.

Once I'm at the bottom of his building, in the fresh air, I stop for a moment and look up at the sky. This is it, I'm completely caught up. I'm going to have to lie to my parents when they ask me how my day went, and refuse their invitation to dinner so as not to have to face my father's gaze. The look of one who knows, one who may suspect everything.

I now feel like a real prostitute. A whore, I've become a whore. Because I know that I'll do it again; that Julien, Joe and Pierre won't change a thing. I've become a whore who, from now on, relies on the money of her customers so she doesn't have to worry about the end of the month. I'm the girl who, for a few hours, knows how to forget the hands that rest on her body. A part-time debauchee, a student whore, a computer whore. In the open air, I regain my color. Slowly, heart racing, I make my way to the nearest bus stop.

Chapter 14

Nervousness

January 14, 2007

Walking in the cold, my coat pulled up to my chin, I run so as not to be late for my first university exam. I'm stressing about today, because I'm taking a literature test. I've read all the books, of course, but I'm very late: I couldn't buy them, given their prohibitive price, and had to wait until they were available in the college library.

This was only the case last week, when I had to swallow three books in quick succession. I had learned my lessons stupidly beforehand, because without having read the works, they obviously seemed meaningless to me. So last week was full of adrenalin. I was running between my job, my studies, the transport to get to university, with the added stress of exams. But today, for the first test, I'm in a state of anxiety. I run through the university corridors to get to the building where the exam is taking place. When I arrive, there's already a small crowd in front of the lecture hall. When you've been running since you jumped out of bed, once you stop moving, you suddenly realize how tired you are. Only nervousness keeps me on my feet.

Two days earlier, I had seen a customer. This time, I'd decided to save some of my loot for a little treat: I'd go shopping. That's the problem with fast money. You always want more.

So I went to see a guy. He was only looking for someone to "do household chores in a state of undress". With exams coming up, I still needed the money, but I was nervously less willing to put up with being touched. So I spent two hours at this guy's place ironing his shirts in my underwear, that's all. He gave me 100 euros.

On the subway to university, this fresh story came back to my mind and I suddenly felt dirtier than ever. I know that midterms aren't the best time to develop self-esteem, but I couldn't help hating myself, telling myself I couldn't do it. Prostitution became a drug as soon as the salary from my telemarketing job wasn't enough. When I realized how much money I could make, I even considered giving up phone calls, and "devoting" myself solely to prostitution. I'd only have to work a few hours a month to earn triple my current salary.

But this telemarketing job, as boring and badly paid as it is, is still, along with university, the only thing that keeps me in touch with reality, with real life. If I only kept my job as a prostitute, I tell myself that I'd soon fall headlong into a network, with a pimp in control. He'd make me drop out of college, and I'd become his full-time golden goose.

Outside the amphitheatre, the pressure is mounting. I've got to calm down if I don't want to lose my nerve in front of the exam paper. I reassure myself as best I can: my reaction is normal, it's my first university exam and I'm so passionate about my studies that I feel there's a lot at stake. The week is punctuated by midterms, and I have to keep up the pressure. The only test I'm not afraid of is the oral exam, because I've always found it easy to express myself. I just need to get rid of the literature; once I've passed that test, I'll be more relaxed.

I rummage in my coat pocket for my rolled tobacco. I'm down to crumbs. So, as usual, I ask my college girlfriend if she'll kindly lend me a cigarette. Luxury, a real cigarette before an exam, can only be a good sign!

The amphitheatre doors open and I enter, determined to show what I can do.

Chapter 15

The Meeting

January 24, 2007

Paul's bar has naturally become my stronghold. I discovered it a long time ago, long before I was a student. I immediately felt at home. The decor is made of dark wood, in the colonial style. There are many photos of actresses from the '40s on the walls, and even though I didn't know most of them, they quickly became familiar to me. I don't go back that often, though, because I want the same magic in my eyes every time. Paul nods to me as I pass by from time to time, and we exchange a few words. At first, I'd take refuge there when my "professional" appointments were over. Then I started coming here more and more regularly: before or after work, for a coffee or an impromptu chat with random friends.

Its importance in my life only took a radical turn the day I took refuge there after my first time with Joe. Since that day, the bar has evoked for me relief, sweetness after emotional and physical violence. I drown my dark thoughts and melancholy there, forgetting my whole life. It's a transitional place between hotels and my apartment: I've formed a real cocoon here.

In the course of my visits to the bar, I've made friends with Paul, the waiter. I enjoy his presence. I talk to him without fear, but never go into details. This is partly because I don't want to: I'm not the kind of girl who tells her life story to the first person who comes along. Secondly, Paul is a rather superficial person. He wouldn't have been interested in any of my stories, except for my sex stories. Nothing annoys me more than someone you talk to who looks around, desperately looking for something to hold his gaze on. Given how little I trust him as a "solemn keeper of secrets to life and death", I've definitely crossed off the possibility of confessing anything about my forbidden games. Revealing such a secret is still unthinkable. I don't want to have to justify myself, not to have to face his gaze which, without going so far as to judge me, couldn't help feeling sorry for me. Come to think of it, I don't think he would have believed me.

Paul is a lady-killer. Overly ego-driven, he hits on everyone who walks into his bar. Express conquests. He bangs them, then dumps them a few days or even hours later. In fact, he tried his luck with me at the very beginning. I think he made it his business to seduce every cute girl who came through the door. He talked me up quite a bit, but I'm clearly not interested in him: in my mind, he's too closely linked to my life as a prostitute. He sensed this and quickly crossed me off his prey list. I don't think he was really interested in me. In his eyes, I would have just been another conquest, and he wasn't willing, any more for me than for anyone else, to row to his ends. He's not the type to struggle for a girl. I also keep telling myself that, being so geographically close to my mysterious meeting places, he'll eventually understand, if he really wants to, what I'm doing and where I'm going.

At the height of my life as a prostitute, this place became my second home. I have to admit that the clientele has a lot to do with it. Most of them are in their thirties: fresh businessmen or fallen artists, sometimes models, this bar exudes youth. All these people mingle happily in the bar, transforming the hubbub of voices into a harmonious din.

I've always felt more mature than other girls my age, and in conversations with complete strangers - but complete strangers in their thirties - I've found that I feel most at home with this age group. I was forced to grow up faster than others when I was a child, and my parents always raised me to be as responsible as possible. As a result, I had a hard time putting up with the childishness of high school. While they amused me at times, the speeches of my fellow girls often made me sit up and take notice. The recurring "You don't know what? My boyfriend at the time was thirty and had had a car for quite some time. So nothing out of the ordinary for me. I couldn't bring myself to take part in their weekend sleepovers or their first experiments with so-called light drugs.

As a rule, I came to school to take my classes and left just as quickly. I rarely mingled with the other students. Without being haughty, I naturally distanced myself from the group. I enjoyed their presence for a day, but never "dug in" or tried to see them again outside school. The same was true of guys.

As far back as I can remember, boys my age have always deeply bored me, apart from Manu, who's about the same generation as me. When I was old enough to flirt, I never considered them as potential boyfriends. I prefer accomplished men, who are no longer in a post-adolescent crisis or in search of an identity.

Sometimes I regret having grown up so fast, because in high school I felt alone, misunderstood, out of step with time and experiences. I think like a thirty-something, my thoughts are ten years older than I am. In the end, I wish I'd been able to have fun like a girl my age, superficially, without constantly thinking like a responsible adult. I sometimes feel tired of my own nature, but I can't help it: I have to admit that I'll never be a person who enjoys childish things, even temporarily. I lost my naivety a long time ago.

That's one of the reasons why I immediately felt at home in Paul's bar. I come alone almost all the time, certain to end the evening chatting with new faces.

Tonight, when I arrive, I find the place packed. A rock concert has been organized and a bunch of tipsy customers have turned the bar into a real dance floor. The good mood is infectious and I find myself smiling as soon as I cross the threshold. Paul spots me and hastens to pour me a glass of wine, to "put me at ease" he says. In fact, I know he wants to show off to the guys at the bar who have been staring at me for a long time while I kissed him. It's his way of saying: "Hey, guys, I know her…".

It worked. Two men immediately tried to strike up a conversation with me.

- Hi, do you come to this bar often?" says one, not very original.

- I've never seen you there, and I know I wouldn't miss a pretty girl like you!" says the other, inspired.

What creativity! Their approach smacks of low-level flirting: I can smell a man's sexual desire a hundred yards away. I kindly answer their questions. I even allow myself a few flat initiatives, purely out of politeness. The two zigotos know each other well, and before my very eyes, the discussion turns into a competition. Who will take the young lady home tonight? It's up to the one who puts the biggest smile on my face. I try to remain cordial, but I'm dying to leave them there, to make them understand once and for all that they don't stand a chance with me.

Suddenly, I notice him behind the two men. He's been looking at me for several minutes. Dark-haired, a few strands of hair hide his eyes, which I can only guess are green. He's wearing a striped cotton shirt, rolled up at the sleeves. A very average outfit, but despite everything, from the moment I notice him, I can't take my eyes off his. He's a captivating man. He looks at me with a sympathetic eye. It's not the first time I've seen him here. I've seen him chatting with Paul over coffee several times. I smile, thinking I'll never be able to say the famous "Do you come here often?

His eyes give me a sign I don't have time to understand. Two seconds later, he's beside me, grabbing me by the waist in front of my two flirtatious companions. Needless to say, they straighten up rather abruptly, ashamed of having misunderstood me so much. There's a silence, punctuated by their short coughs that betray their embarrassment.

The Meeting

- Ah… hello," managed to stammer one of them.

Two pleasantries later, they're long gone. The savior turns my body towards his, without letting go of my waist. The situation is frighteningly erotic, and I feel a shiver run through me, making the hairs on my arms stand on end. I can't take my eyes off him, while he stares at me wordlessly. He really isn't what you'd call handsome, yet he fascinates me. I could have stayed like this for an hour, but after a good minute, I decide to break the silence:

- Thanks, they were getting rather annoying.

- Yes, that's what I understand.

He points to a table that has just become available. He orders us two glasses of beer, and just like that, we spend the evening together, laughing a lot and chatting about our little lives. His name is Olivier. He doesn't do much in life and seems bored with it. He has the look and lifestyle of a bohemian. For lack of a time machine, this guy seems resigned to the idea of not being able to go back to the 70s. He was born in the wrong era.

The night is light and I feel perfectly fine. I don't know why things seem so easy tonight. Nor can I explain how sometimes you can feel so at ease with a complete stranger… to the point of telling him very intimate things. I tell him about my family, my studies and Manu. He listens attentively, telling me about moments and experiences that have marked him in his childhood or recently. It's a healthy, fair exchange where everyone gives of themselves. Everything is done with a smile, and even suffering is evoked as a constructive step.

One drink follows another as the night progresses. We start to get drunker and drunker, which brings us back to the logic of drunkenness, which is to blithely and unabashedly reveal one's life. I have the strange impression of being able to tell him everything, even and especially what I hide from everyone else. On several occasions, I find myself wondering how he'd react if I confessed my debauched life to him. He's the one who opens the ball of unlimited confessions.

- You see, after thirty years, I feel that today, nothing can shock me. Sad, isn't it?

The perch is too big and my secret too heavy for me to carry alone.

- Nothing can shock you? Is that so?

- Really.

- I'm sure I can shock you.

With the help of alcohol, I'm becoming increasingly adventurous. I know I'm playing with fire, but a strange instinct compels me to trust him. He remains silent for a moment, as if looking for a reply. He understands that this is something I'm still reluctant to confess. Then he says:

- If you're sure, I'm listening.

He senses my indecision. Revealing my hidden life to him means trusting him completely and counting on his loyalty to keep the secret. But I don't know him! How and why should I trust him? Looking at him deeply, I guess he won't say anything. Nevertheless, a glimmer of lucidity still blocks me.

- Don't worry about a thing. This is just between you and me, I promise.

So I take the plunge. I turn the words over and over in my head to get them into a proper verbal form, because they've never been spoken aloud before.

- You know where I was last week?

He nods. He obviously can't know.

- I was with a fifty-year-old man who paid me to touch myself. I'm a prostitute.

I spit it out without thinking. When it's already done, I recoil, as if I've just heard someone else speak.

For a second, his eyes become more piercing, the top of his face frowns but, remembering his promise, he hastens to assume an expression that is meant to be neutral.

- I see," he said simply.

He doesn't put a hand on my shoulder, nor does he make any gesture of compassion that would have exasperated me. On the contrary, he just wants to understand, and asks me lots of questions. The rest of the night is just like the beginning: my revelation hasn't spoiled the evening at all, on the contrary, it's brought us closer together.

Paul jolts us out of our reverie, which has lasted almost six hours. Six straight hours in which nothing existed around us. I haven't seen the time go by at all and think it's a joke when I see Paul arrive, mop in hand, ready to clean up before closing time.

- We have to take off, we're closing!

We burst out laughing, both realizing we've lost track of time. He stands up and offers me his hand to lead me outside. Drunk and hilarious, I greet Paul with an evasive wave of my hand. Outside, Olivier walks me home, supporting me by the waist as my gait zigzags. From start to finish, we have an inexplicable, alcohol-induced laugh. Once at my door, he checks that I've got my keys and can open the door properly. Then, in a slow gesture, he kisses me on the cheek.

I look at him with a smile and go upstairs to sleep, alone but happy.

Chapter 16

Up the Spiral

February 4, 2007

My birthday is fast approaching. I'm going to be 19. "A great age in everyone's eyes. But I'm indifferent to the number on the clock.

19 years old. Two love affairs - one in progress - a literary baccalaureate in her pocket, a university year that's going better than expected, and a hidden life as a prostitute. Not bad for a 19-year-old. Barely 19 years. Yet I feel ten years older.

I'm almost 19 and still in dire need of money. The balance sheets are not good, far from it. My tiny cell phone plan has been confiscated by my telephone operator. I have financial priorities, like my rent, which I'm already struggling to pay. Most of the time, I cheat on the metro to get to university, unable to afford the luxury transport card.

I try to look on the bright side. I'm passionate about my studies: it's been four months now since I joined the vast circle of students, and I'm really enjoying it. Even when I'm tired, I go to class happy, aware of the chance I have to study (almost) for free. My thirst for learning never dries up, and I'm certain that I've found my calling in studying modern languages. My teachers encourage me, and one of them even confided in me recently that he saw in me a future agrégée in languages.

What's more, I got the results of my January mid-term exams. I passed with an average of 15! I couldn't believe it when I got my transcript in the mail. Just goes to show, there is such a thing as justice. I didn't work for nothing.

My small budget obviously prevents me from buying all the books I need. The library has become one of my favorite places, where I like to stroll around and kill time with precious books. But it's not very big, and it was often raided before I arrived, at least in terms of the books on the shelves. However, these repeated minor inconveniences don't make me lose my natural aplomb; they just slow down my learning curve. I envy the young students who go straight to the local bookshop to order books in the original language, holding out their credit cards with a serene smile.

I'm also dying to own a laptop, because it's simply becoming indispensable. This idea was first born in the telemarketing company. One of the employees told us that there would be a prize draw for a laptop. I can only imagine my reaction to this announcement. I visit computer sales pages on the Internet every chance I get and salivate at the technological marvels. Theoretically, I've chosen the one I like best, knowing full well that my parents will never be able to afford it, even for my birthday.

I feel helpless in the face of my daily life. Just over a month ago, I met Joe for the first time. In the space of a month,

I've taken on three major customers, who have helped me temporarily get out of the red, bringing in over 600 euros. Thanks to them, I've been able to solve my biggest financial problems, the ones that had been dragging on for a long time, but I'm still left with rent, bills, etc. I can't see the end of it. I can't see the end of it. Too many things to think about, to sort out. I feel overwhelmed.

I'm taking over my ads on the Net.

First, I contact an amateur photographer. The guy makes me wear the most improbable outfits: even in my most daring fantasies, I couldn't have imagined such accoutrements! As the session progressed, the guy seemed more and more suspicious. He becomes demanding, almost violent in his comments if I don't do what he wants.

- Come on, Laura, don't stand like that! Do you think you can make anyone want you in that position? Don't be so slutty! Be more sexual, yes, like that, with your mouth open, fine!

I cut the session short. As I pocketed the money, I realized that it didn't come close to what I could make from sleeping with a stranger. Besides, I'm not at all comfortable with the concept: photos leave marks. I'm not ready to take such risks. I want to be as discreet as possible. The guy calls me back several times, even suggesting threesomes with another girl.

- You'll see, she's a student like you, and the two of you will really hit it off, I'm sure!

The mere idea of ending up with another poor girl in the same shit as me makes my blood run cold. He senses my reluctance and so increases his rates, more and more tempting, reaching unbelievable amounts for a young girl like me. However, I'm certain that if I accept, I'll fall into this guy's clutches. He has all the characteristics of the perfect pimp: sweet and protective, violent the next. He seems to be part of a very extensive network on V. If I let him near me, I'll never get out of prostitution. I can't see my future in it, and neither can any prostitute.

Being so close to the vortex of these networks makes me shudder: I feel both frail and powerless in the face of these manipulators; but also strong for managing to keep my head on my shoulders. So far, I've managed to spot the danger in time, and not accept just anything. I've been able to avoid the pimps, but how long will I last? Once you've become a prostitute, no matter what happens, you're in an environment where people know and recognize you. I don't have a penny to my name, and it seems that the deeper I get into this hidden life, the harder it becomes to make ends meet. Every time I have a financial problem, I'm tempted to turn to prostitution. The vicious circle is there, taunting me and dragging me into its vortex: the more money I earn, the more I spend and the more I want.

I know I've been "lucky" so far. Nobody has forced me, I haven't run into any raving lunatics. I sometimes tremble when I realize this: maybe I'm waiting for something much more shocking to happen to me before I put an end to this double life. What if that trigger doesn't happen? What if the limits are pushed back little by little, so gradually that I don't feel the danger coming? Will I one day become one of the so-called "professionals"? Will I have the strength to pull through?

I rarely allow myself to think about it. Not out of denial: I'm fully aware that I'm playing with fire. I'm only trying to protect myself. At the moment, I haven't found any other way of getting money quickly, so I might as well try not to dwell too much on what's happening to me.

All these negative assessments are fuelling my schizophrenia. I feel myself splitting into two as I think. Neither all black, nor all white; neither a complete prostitute, nor a complete student, my life contradicts itself in every way. The rest of the time, I firmly believe in the future. I see myself with a small family in a beautiful house, a job I love, far away from all this crap. I know I have the resources to get back on track. I'll get through this, that's for sure. Later, I'll keep this secret feeling of success, of victory. Where few girls have succeeded, I'll set an example.

Later, I've made up my mind, I'm going to be a good person. At this point in my life, I can't afford it.

I began to consider the Joe solution more and more seriously. Since our first meeting, he hasn't let me go. I receive e-mails from him every day, which I automatically delete without even reading. New to the business, I can't imagine ever seeing the same customers again. I soon realize that it's precisely these customers that we have to rely on, as they represent a real lifeline in the most precarious moments of our lives as prostitutes.

I guess I'm stupidly hoping for a *Pretty Woman* scenario, where a Richard Gere lookalike comes along and gets me out of all this hell. I keep telling myself that it won't happen if I keep seeing the same customers over and over again. So

I look elsewhere for the rare pearl, avoiding Joe like the plague. It makes me smile that even for one customer, I'm dreaming of some kind of Prince Charming.

But Richard Gere is a long time coming, and when I receive a new letter from my landlady demanding rent within the week, I tell myself that I can find clients anywhere, without any problems. It's not so easy to find customers I know I can trust. The ads often exude a perversity that prevents me from making contact with them. Joe is different. My last impression of him is that I've taken him for a ride. He cheerfully paid me for practically nothing: just rubbing his hands all over my body. His fantasies now seem quite manageable. I forget all the hateful sensations that accompanied this encounter, all the embarrassment and disgust I felt. I can't see it yet, but that's exactly where the danger lies: remembering only the envelope full of money.

My landlady's letter was followed the next day by my pay slip. I grimaced as I discovered the total amount of my salary: radishes, that's what I'm making with this teleoperator job.

I contact Joe that evening from an Internet cafe, initially just asking for news. This guy must live in front of his PC, because he answers me within a second.

In the second e-mail, I tell him I'm willing to see him soon, but the sooner the better, as I need money very quickly. Obviously, he's in a hurry to accept, pressed by his desire. But out of politeness and courtesy, he asks about me anyway. I slip into my reply that my birthday is coming up and that perhaps we could get together that day. Without hesitation, I include the Internet page of my dream computer as an attachment.

I realize that my approach is shocking to many. I tell myself that since these perverts want my ass, they'll pay good money for it. But I can't resign myself to the status of "prostitute": for me, I'm better than that. And money is the only way I can prove it to myself. My 19th birthday is coming up, and this year more than any other, I need support, comfort. I stupidly think I can find it in a computer offered by a client. How stupid I can be!

The e-mail he sends me afterwards isn't as quick. I know I've upset him a bit. But how can he believe for a second that I'm contacting him again because I like him? I'm only interested in his money. He answers anyway, asking me why I need a computer. I explain that a computer would greatly simplify my daily life as a student. I give him a lot of flattery, because I know I'm dealing with a protective dad, and he's easily softened. I receive his reply a few minutes later:

Laura,

Apparently, times are tough for you right now. I completely understand why you need a computer. Which model are you interested in? Do you have a particular preference?…

I know right then and there that the case is in the bag. I don't even feel ashamed. I think at this moment, I'm ready to accept anything from him, convinced that our future meeting will be my last experience as a prostitute.

He goes ahead and sets up an appointment within three days. On my birthday.

Chapter 17

The Fall

February 7, 2007

At 1 p.m. I'm waiting for him outside the same hotel as the first time. We're going to spend two hours together, as I have to leave for work afterwards. Pierre's episode is still very much with me, and my eyes dart around frantically in all directions. I try to watch everyone passing by undetected, hoping that Joe will arrive soon. Ironically, I only feel comfortable when I'm alone with him in the room. I know that no passer-by is fooled by seeing us together on the street.

I remember talking to a prostitute one day, without revealing my "shadow profession". She told me that on the sidewalk, she keeps in touch with her "colleagues" by telephone every half-hour. As soon as one of them gets into a car, she warns her colleagues to intervene if they don't see her return. The students, most of whom operate via the Net, are ultimately far more exposed to danger alone in a bedroom than on the sidewalk.

I can see him in the distance, still armed with his magician's case. We kiss, and he says to me:

- Go up to the room before me.

- Why?

- Since the last time with the cops, I'd rather we tried to be more discreet. You never know. Ask at reception for the keys. I didn't know your last name, so I gave mine.

Of course he doesn't know my name! And there's no way he ever will.

- Then go upstairs and settle in, and I'll meet you there in a moment.

By *settle down*, he means put on the sexy clothes he's asked me to bring with me. I nod and head for reception. A young woman is there. She looks up at me, a professional smile on her lips.

When I get to the front of the room, I put my ear to the ground to see if I can hear anything inside. I'm sure I hear moaning, but I'm getting suspicious now. Someone may be waiting for me, and that someone wants to hurt me. I literally stick my ear to the white wood of the door. I quickly conclude that my limitless imagination is playing tricks on me, and that I need to stop being paranoid. I turn the key in the lock.

When I open the door, it's the green curtains that first greet me. Just like the first time, I'm struck by their ugliness. The room may be smaller, but the decor is identical, so my bearings remain more or less the same. For the moment, things haven't really changed. Strangely, this reassures me.

I discover a laptop sitting on a small table opposite the bed. A pornographic film is displayed in full screen: I'm relieved to know I wasn't dreaming: the moans are coming from there. A note lies on the bed. Again, Joe hasn't changed. Leaving letters for his expensive lovers is undeniably one of his fantasies.

Laura,

I'm very happy to see you again today. I'd like you to start by taking a shower. Then I'll come and knock three times on the door. I want you to say, "Come in, master."

Afterwards, you'll lie down on the bed. I want you to say, "Hello, master, everything you see is yours."

How ridiculous! He's redoubling his domineering fantasies. I'm starting to get scared, and the tone of the session is moving away from the last time, when Joe took a lot of flack.

At no point in his letter does he mention the computer. "*Just this once, Laura, it will be the last*," I say to myself.

I approach the device slowly, observing it. I begin to wonder if it's for me or if Joe is just taunting me. I feel he's capable of anything. I caress the keys slowly, full of envy but still wondering if I'm really ready to accept anything to possess it. What if this computer isn't for me? What if he decides not to give it to me in the end? My mind is focused solely on this possession, my desire has turned into an immeasurable need. I want this computer at all costs.

I decide to take a shower to clear my head. A pleasant surprise awaits me in the bathroom: there's no mirror. I don't think I'd have been able to face my image today, on my 19th birthday, when I'm about to sell my body to buy a computer. I take a quick shower. I'm still drying off when I hear Joe banging on the door. I stand in the middle of the room, naked, and say to him:

- Come in, master.

I couldn't help laughing when I heard myself say that. I imagine him smiling with pleasure behind the door. Instead, he comes in, stares at me for a few seconds and says curtly:

- We're not kidding.

I'm sure he feels that, given his expensive gift, he can afford to be more demanding with me. "*Okay, sweetie, don't get too smart today… Play along, there's a computer at stake…*", I say to myself inwardly. I'm really obsessed with the device. Joe interrupts my reverie:

- Lie across the bed on your stomach, widthways.

I now comply without flinching, not even daring to open my mouth to speak. In this position, Joe can see my body perfectly, especially my buttocks, which I hate. It's the middle of the afternoon and the light is shining through the green curtains, which in itself isn't particularly surprising given their quality. I'm really not comfortable.

My body is bigger than the width of the bed, so my head and feet stick out at the ends. Joe notices this and says to me:

- Drop your head into the void and run your hands under the bed.

I do it without really understanding what he's getting at, just hoping he won't then ask me to put my left leg over my head and do a headstand. I feel a cold piece of cardboard under the bed. I pull the box towards me to get it out of its hiding place so I can look at it.

A laptop. My laptop. I can't help smiling at the sight of it. I suddenly become demonic in my head: now that I have my present, why sleep with him? But how can I imagine for a second that Joe will let me go like this?

Joe's not that stupid. He must have seen the spark of mischief in my eye, because he suddenly says to me:

- Of course, you can open it later.

So I'm going through with it, there's no escaping it. I've just realized that he's also going to pay me for today. I smile at my future wealth. I'm also genuinely moved: this computer is the most expensive gift I've ever been given. I haven't been given much in life without expecting something in return. Joe obviously gives me financially, but today he gave me a glimpse of another side of his personality that was unknown to me until now: his human, generous side. At least that's what I tell myself.

The vicious circle is established: he manipulates me, but I don't realize it. Joe knows what he's doing. He wants me and knows he has to bait me with money. The boundaries between us have been pushed once again. Joe pulls the reins.

He asks me to sit on the bed beside him. He turns up the sound of the film he's just paused on the computer. It's an amateur sadomasochistic film showing a nude woman in her forties, rather plump, having her body burned with a candle. She's tied to the chair she's sitting on, the wax drips onto her breasts and she screams to death. The more she screams, the more the awful man responsible for her pain takes pleasure. In the end, she too seems to be enjoying herself. As the images pass before my eyes without registering on my retina, I actually find it hard to watch these scenes.

I regularly watch pornographic films. Out of curiosity, to heighten the excitement, I sometimes watch them with my friends or my boyfriend, just like everyone else. Sadomasochism is totally different. I don't think I'll ever understand the appeal of films in this category. After two minutes, I already find the scene unbearable and am forced to look away. I've turned into an ice cube watching these images. Joe, on the other hand, is having the time of his life.

- Frankly, Joe, I can't watch, it's not my thing at all.

- The problem is, it's mine, so I'm not asking you to look.

The tone is radically different from last time. He has total contempt for me: I've been reduced to the level of a cheap whore who's only there to offer her ass and keep her mouth shut.

- What I suggest is that you tie your hands to the bed.

I immediately made the connection with the video. Does he want to burn me too? And I thought I'd be safer with him in the hotel room!… Joe softens a little.

- Don't worry, Laura.

Gently, he approaches me. He slowly tilts my body into a recumbent position, then straightens me onto my side. He then joins my wrists behind my back and ties them with my sweater, which is lying on the bed. The knot isn't really tight, which reassures me a little, because I can free myself if I want to.

Joe doesn't seem willing to let me have it. He grabs a string out of nowhere and binds my ankles, still behind my back.

Then, to be on the safe side, he ties my feet and wrists together. I must be like a piece of cold meat at the butchers. Why do I let this happen to me?

He then takes a dildo out of his briefcase. It's not the first time I've seen one in real life, but this one seems bigger. At the sight of the object, I shudder and let out a moan of fear. Joe doesn't react. He couldn't care less now that I'm tied up.

Captive. I'm at her fucking mercy now.

He walks over to me and stuffs a tissue in my mouth, finishing it off with a blindfold around my head. He has rendered me immobile and mute in two minutes without my being able to react. I feel powerless, repeating to myself in anguish: "*Even if it hurts, I won't be able to scream.*"

With the help of lubricant and his supernatural object, Joe manages to excite me physically. Then comes the horror and pain. The first blow is unspeakably painful.

I let out a cry that remains muffled in the tissue. It doesn't stop, on the contrary. I scream inaudible "Stop!", tears streaming down my face as the pain is so unbearable. As far as possible, I slam my thighs together to make him understand that he has to stop. I wriggle around so much that it's impossible for him to hold me or insert anything inside me. What's more, my mooing must be starting to be heard from outside. Panic-stricken by this trance, he finally unties the blindfold and ties, offering me a new freedom. As soon as the last knot is undone, I leap to my feet. I turn around slowly, my hair totally disheveled, my breathing still panting. I must look like a fury. I'm looking straight at him now. I feel like murder.

He just looks at me sheepishly, well aware of my psychological state. But once again, the situation pleases him. At the sight of my reddened, bloodshot eyes, he plays innocent:

- Well then? I thought you liked submission…

Even he doesn't believe it anymore. I don't answer but throw on my clothes and start to get dressed at top speed. Who knows what he's still capable of!… I've seen enough for today. For ever, in fact.

- Are you leaving? We agreed on two hours. You still have an hour to spend with me.

Afraid he'll turn violent, I decide to make up an excuse. He probably won't believe it, but it doesn't matter, I've got to go. Hands trembling, I find the strength to babble at breakneck speed:

- It's my birthday today, so I'm not going to work after all. My friends are waiting for me in a café to celebrate with a drink. I'm in the middle of midterms too, so I won't be able to stay long with them, as I have to go home afterwards to study.

I give him as many excuses as I can, telling myself that out of this pack of lies, one is bound to slip through. I feel my body and head on the verge of an anxiety attack, I've got to get out of here fast before I go crazy in this filthy hotel room. Money or no money, I'm getting out of this place.

Joe then uses the last arguments likely to persuade me to stay a little longer. He plays the apology card.

- Don't take it that way, Laura, it was just a little fantasy.

- A little fantasy? Well, it's definitely not mine…

I stop there, seeing no point in talking to him any more. I'm now fully dressed and putting on my coat when Joe says:

- Aren't you going to have a shower?

My reply is curt:

- No, I'm leaving.

I've broken several of his commandments at once, and he's unsettled and doesn't know how to react. I don't want to give him time to think about it; my hand is already on the door handle. I retrace my steps for a second, aware that I've forgotten something. Without a glance at him, I grab the laptop, tuck it under my arm and head out the door, as fast as I can.

In the corridor, Joe catches up with me.

- Here, Laura, you forgot this too.

He hands me an envelope. The same as last time. I open it… to discover 400 euros inside. He puts his hand to my head as I raise my face to him. My features are more tense than ever. He strokes my hair and says:

- It was good, I liked it.

He says it in a "good girl" tone, which makes me nauseous again. I practically snatch the envelope out of his hand and run off without looking back.

I run out of the hotel breathless. Tears roll down my cheeks but almost turn to ice in the winter cold. I can't be alone. I head straight for my favorite bar, the one that welcomed me when, after the first time, I didn't feel like going home.

Paul is there, behind the counter, wiping down his hundredth drink of the day. He sees me rush in, cheeks rosy with cold, eyes shining. I have no intention of confiding my woes to him; no one must ever know. My appearance is not normal; he wouldn't believe it if I told him everything was fine. My face reflects extreme panic: the only way out is to pretend that this disorder is pleasant.

- Laura? Is everything all right?" he asks as I sit down in a high chair at the bar.

- Yes, very good. Something crazy has just happened to me! On this point, I'm not fooling him. "*Quick, invent something.*

- I just won this laptop at work! Isn't it great?

Ah, that's a good excuse! I'm doing fine. I show him my hard-earned object. Inwardly, I award myself the best liar of the year flag. Paul congratulates me, obviously delighted for me. I order him a coffee, and without having to ask, he tells me the latest neighborhood gossip. Perfect, talking or thinking would have been a terrible effort for me right now.

After a few minutes, I cut him off:

- Paul, tell me, do you mind if I take a shower?

- No, not at all, make yourself at home.

I couldn't have stayed another minute with Joe's scent on my skin, and since I'm offered the chance to wash up, I jump at it. I make my way through the back room to reach the floor where the bathroom is, the computer still under my arm. The grime and shame are embedded in my body, and it's going to take a lot of scrubbing to get it all off.

I let the water run for a long time over my body, and use half the shower gel. When I come out, I still feel as dirty as ever. Suddenly, everything changes. I see the computer in the corner of the room and something crazy happens that I couldn't have imagined a second earlier: I smile. I'm simply happy to know that it's now mine. Joy takes over and any fears I may have had on leaving the hotel gently melt away. I feel light and ready to face life again. What's more, it's my birthday, and I don't want to spoil the day with gloomy thoughts - there's plenty of time to mope later. I never thought I'd be smiling this afternoon.

I gather my things, say goodbye to Paul one last time and leave the bar with a seemingly tranquil mind. I head for work. I don't even think I'm despicable for being happy about this object.

Happy birthday, Laura.

Chapter 18

Love

March 2007

Although nothing materialized between us, Olivier and I continued to see each other in parallel with my forbidden extracurricular activities. Our relationship is platonic. In any case, it's not a formal relationship. I try to convince myself, to calm my impatience, that I prefer this situation. We're both afraid of what might happen if we try to kiss. Several times a week, we meet after work and very often in Paul's bar, where we first met.

I don't know what he does for a living, as he always seems to be available for appointments and regularly offers them on his own. I figure he must be on the dole. A comparison with my ex-partner Manu is inevitable. I've gone from being a tightwad to someone who certainly doesn't have a lot of money, but who takes me out to dinner whenever he can. I've never even kissed him, but I know he's an important part of my life.

We never talk about my underground life as a problem to be solved. Olivier seems to have accepted the idea that he's interested in a girl who sells her body to pay for her studies. I confess I've long since lost the thread of clear, precise thought about this part of my life. Olivier doesn't ask me anything either. He probably has other demons to fight before he can tackle mine.

We spend whole days together, wandering around V., or long evenings chatting at my place until dawn. We understand each other easily, sometimes disagree, but our relationship is incredibly human: one always tries to grasp the other's thoughts before criticizing them. We also have a lot of fun together. His laughter is a delight to my ears and eyes. The second before it explodes into the air, I guess he's ready to leap to his lips, which pull back into an improvised grimace before finally relaxing completely. I look at him then and forget to laugh myself, captivated by this surprising tableau. This guy isn't handsome, but in my eyes, he's magnificent. Far from perfect, and that's what makes him so noble. He then stops joking to admire me in turn, and silence falls, natural and beautiful.

I still can't believe how little time it took us to get so close. I'm not looking for a long explanation; life and its encounters don't always have one. I've often worked this way, letting myself be carried along by events, accepting them as they come and trying, as far as possible, not to complain.

One evening, he calls to ask me to dinner at his place. I happily accept, his presence becoming more and more essential to me; I literally miss him as soon as I leave him.

The evening passes without surprises, in good spirits. We're happy to meet up again, even though we saw each other the day before. The discussion takes its usual course: a clatter of nonsense, a hustle and bustle of jokes mixed with more serious subjects. Then, at the end of the meal, Olivier takes his glass of red wine in hand and bangs his knife on the edge of the plate with a noise that demands silence. His face is rather serious, and since it's a look I don't know him for, I stiffen a little in my chair.

- Laura…

He's still searching for words, is that a good sign? I don't answer, I'm not interested.

- Laura…

Then he slowly gets up to kiss me. It's the most beautiful declaration of love I've ever received. I've heard my first name so often in recent months, distorted by the furious desires of strangers. I even wished I'd never heard it again, so much has it pushed my schizophrenia to the limit, forcing me to juggle with my new imaginary friend, the new roommate of my brain: Laura the prostitute.

But here, my whole identity finds its place and its raison d'être. I'm not a whore in his eyes, I'm Laura. This kiss clarifies what we've been afraid to admit all these weeks: we're passionately in love. After Manu, I never thought I'd fall in love again so quickly, given my hidden life. Of course, I don't have any feelings with my customers, and as a result, it seemed to me that I'd become hermetically sealed off from all emotion. Tonight, Olivier proves me wrong. With this kiss, insignificant to many, I feel alive again, I accept myself as a loving being and no longer just as an object at the service of strangers.

The weeks that followed were the most intense of my short life. Olivier and I never leave each other's side, we go through life together, with no questions asked about the future. I continue to see clients, simply because I still need the money. I've become increasingly demanding in my lifestyle, allowing myself to afford things I couldn't have imagined myself owning six months ago.

The first time we make love, something very revealing happens. In the middle of the action, Olivier pauses to look deeply into my green eyes. He suddenly breaks the silence to say:

- Laura…

He swallows his saliva, as if plucking up the courage to speak.

- Laura, what are you doing here?

- Uh, I'm here with you. We're making love.

- No, Laura. Now you're letting me fuck you, it's not the same.

I recoiled.

- Laura, I'm not fucking you. I'm making love to you.

I stop and think for a moment about what Olivier has just told me. After all these months of having only my clients for sexuality, I didn't realize that I'd adopted certain reflexes to protect myself. Waiting, not moving, closing my eyes: all this is obviously not compatible with a boyfriend.

Olivier gives me a long hug and I fall into a deep, peaceful, serene sleep. The next day, we make love with magnificent gentleness.

Olivier doesn't turn a blind eye to my forbidden life - on the contrary. Over time, he's become my diary: I always inform him of the time and place of my appointments, in case anything should happen to me. I don't realize how strange this relationship is. He literally allows me to cheat on him and, worse, helps me with my organization. We don't talk about it afterwards, because he doesn't need to hear what happened. I don't see him as a masochist and I don't see myself as a sadistic girl. We just want to share everything, and if that means he has to know the names of my customers and my appointment times, I'm ready to tell him.

One day, I arrange to meet a new stranger near the station. I'm supposed to meet him in the late afternoon, and before I go, Olivier and I drop into Paul's bar for a coffee. As I swallow the first hot sip of my coffee, my mobile starts ringing. It's the man on the other end of the line.

- Laura? Yes, I'd prefer to meet in the parking lot in front of the station, around 9 p.m. Is that all right? I know it's later than planned, but I've got something to do before then.

- In front of the station? I'm not sure…

This guy's getting suspicious.

- I'm not sure I'd want to meet you there at this time of night.

Olivier has raised his head and is now listening to the conversation.

- But no, don't worry, Laura, I'll be in the car, I'll just pick you up and we'll leave quickly. We're not spending the evening there!

This conversation must stop immediately and this appointment must be cancelled. There's no way I'm meeting a stranger in his car near the station at this late hour.

- I'll have to cancel, I'm not available at this time.

I cut the line without waiting for an answer from him. Olivier hasn't taken his eyes off me, but I'm avoiding them. He senses something is wrong.

- Is everything all right?" he finally asks.

- Yes, everything's fine. I'm canceling this customer.

He hasn't even had time to smile when my cell phone starts ringing again. I should have expected it, this weird guy isn't going to let go any time soon. We contemplate the shrill ringing of the phone. We realize who's calling, and for the first time in our relationship, I feel my forbidden games coming between us.

I answer. Still him.

- Laura, why did you hang up? I'm sure we can meet later, or another day. I mean, we can work something out, can't we?

I stammer that I'm not free, and once again hang up abruptly. Olivier's eyes light up with fury, he's about to explode. I take both his hands and shower them with kisses. We feel the pressure of the situation, waiting for the phone to ring again.

Our silence is effectively broken a few minutes later. In a gesture of extreme violence, Olivier grabs the phone and picks it up, shouting an angry "allô!

I have no idea what the customer said. I guess he got scared by a hateful male voice. I can only watch Olivier bellow at the guy never to call me again, that he'll personally track him down if he tries to contact me again.

I understand we've gone beyond our limits. By shouting, losing his temper, no longer knowing what he's saying, Olivier lets go of the anger he'd been building up, unconsciously or not, over the last few weeks.

After a few seconds of insults, he puts the phone down in a violent gesture on the wooden table. He looks at me for just a second, then looks away to concentrate on his coffee. We never broach the subject again, and I keep my prostitution a secret. No more agendas, no more planning for the two of us, I become his girlfriend again and he decides to turn a blind eye to what he should never have known.

Our passionate relationship is quickly ruined by this episode. Olivier can no longer pretend. As for me, I can't stop: I want more and more money. At this point in my life, losing Olivier is the thing I dread most in the world, but I continue to see clients. Prostitution is also part of my daily life, and I'm convinced that I won't make it financially without it.

One morning, when I woke up at his place, I found the bed empty. The place is still warm and the morning not far advanced. Olivier is in the kitchen, at the window, pensive. He sips his coffee slowly, his gaze devoid of life.

I tiptoe up to him and run my hand lovingly up and down his back. He doesn't react. Then comes what I've been dreading for days now.

- Laura...

Always that "Laura" that comes back, the one he used to declare his love for me, to help me rediscover my identity. But this time, it sounds frighteningly different. That "Laura" is a period, that "Laura" ends our story in that dark kitchen at dawn.

That's all there is to it. I leave the same day, packing up my belongings scattered all over the mess of his apartment. It's only when I'm outside that I let the tears roll down my cheeks. For once, I don't wipe them away; they deserve to stream down my face.

Chapter 19

Panic

March 25, 2007

Leaning against Paul's bar, I chat gently, superficially. I haven't been back here since I broke up with Olivier a week ago. In fact, he carefully avoids the place.

For the first time in my life, I feel alone in the world. A few months ago, I made the choice to confide my heavy secret, and now I feel I can no longer bury it deep inside myself as I used to. It weighs too heavily on me.

Paul is thoughtful enough not to mention Olivier: perhaps out of respect for our silent suffering. Or maybe he just doesn't give a damn. So light, uninteresting conversation naturally becomes our main exchange.

This afternoon, I decided to get out of the house, after a week spent brooding over my pain in the solitude of my apartment, immersed in work. I know I need to forget and move on, but it's much harder than I imagined. I need to get back to a "normal" life, although I can't bring myself to call it that.

The door suddenly opened. The bar isn't very big, and customers who enter are inevitably stared at a little by the customers.

I recognize him immediately. My blood runs cold, I'm petrified. He's accompanied by his girlfriend, who may even be his wife, and to top it all off, there's his child. A smiling blond boy with big blue eyes and gorgeous curls. I only glance quickly at his wife. I can't help it, I have to detail her. She's dark-haired and rather tall, a little chubby but very elegant. She holds her little one by the hand and smiles at him. She must be a good mother.

I quickly turn back to the bar, my back to the door. I don't know what to do.

- Hi, Paul," says the guy.

- Hi, Mathias! How've you been? Long time no see! Ah, you brought the whole family today!

Shit, they know each other! This is hell! A month earlier, this guy contacted me for a "massage" in a shabby hotel. Now I find him in this bar, my bar. I don't dare get up from my stool, not to face him, of course, but also not to realize what's really going on.

Meanwhile, Mathias hasn't yet noticed my presence and is chatting to Paul, while behind my back I can hear Goldilocks chirping to her mother from a distance. Mathias has only seen me once, so perhaps it's understandable that he doesn't recognize my neck. After all, I'm just a pleasant mistake that he quickly forgot. I recognize them all, I know their faces by heart, having watched them a lot. I recognize their voices, and regularly turn around in the street thinking I've heard one of them.

He's literally leaning against the bar now, brushing me with his shoulder. I've got to get out of here, I've got to get out of this bar as quickly as possible. I get down from my chair with my head bowed, and stumble a little over my bag as I put my feet on the floor, causing him to turn around.

Our eyes meet. His mouth drops open. He knows he's seen me somewhere before, and by searching for a second in his head, he's figured out where. I can see the horror and panic in his eyes at seeing me here. We're stuck for just a second, but it feels like an eternity.

Seeing that I'm grabbing my bag and getting ready to leave, Paul asks me:

- Leaving so soon, Laura? You haven't even finished your coffee!

- I've just remembered I've got something to do, I've got to go," I stammered, getting tangled up in the strap of my satchel.

- Wait a minute, come here and meet Mathias, one of my best mates!

"No, I already know your buddy, and quite well at that." Paul can't understand the panic I'm feeling right now. If he were to touch my sweaty hands, he'd know something was wrong. Mathias, for his part, glances frantically at his sweetheart crouched behind him, happily too busy playing with her offspring.

- Hello, nice to meet you, Laura," I say, holding out my hand for him to shake.

- Uh, hi, uh… Mathias, nice to meet you too.

You bet! Our fingers, stiff as stakes, join in a vague, swift handshake. Our anxious glances seek a diversion. Paul notices our discomfort.

- Are you all right, Laura? Don't you want to stay a little longer?

- No, I have to go, sorry.

Oh yes, I'm sorry. Without further ado, I head for the exit, mumbling an inaudible "goodbye". I see the look on Paul's face, who doesn't understand; he simply shrugs and starts wiping his glasses.

I run for a minute or two without stopping, to get this bar and this moment out of my mind. My run ends at the corner of a small street, and I take a huge breath of fresh air. Suddenly, I want to scream and cry at the same time. This is too much: my two lives have met, my two personalities have rubbed shoulders. So far, I've managed to keep things straight, but you can't ask too much of me. I've faced Mathias's family: everything I refuse to imagine when I'm with a client has materialized unbeknownst to me today.

It's no longer possible. I have to leave this town at all costs.

Chapter 20

Deprivation

March 30, 2007

I promised myself I wouldn't see Joe again, but he took me by the scruff of the neck. I informed him of my imminent departure for Paris. I stupidly thought that he would leave me alone. Was I clear in my head? "For your departure to Paris, you need money, you can't leave with nothing in your pockets. Come on, just one last time, it's not much and it suits us both."

I recently got his mobile number and he got mine. I gave it to him under pressure, and now I realize my mistake. To say that he calls me regularly would have been a lie: he's literally stalking me! He really likes me and I fit his fantasy of a sexy, naughty student. And now he's offering me something crazy.

Nothing less than 1,000 euros for five hours. Very attractive indeed. But five hours is a long time. What's he up to? I immediately think of the amount of money involved. I've never been able to get rates like that, and the money would allow me to arrive in Paris more serene. I'd be able to take my time and find a respectable job that suited me, not a quick job in a dingy bar. In my mind, it's out of the question to fall back into a mess like V. I'm clearly running away from this city. I'm clearly running away from this town, I don't want to have to hide, calculate and lie anymore. In Paris, I'll get wise.

We've arranged to meet at the same hotel as usual. I find this place reassuring after all. In spite of everything, a trust, stupid I admit it, binds me to Joe. Sure, he made me howl with pain and humiliation the last time we met, but at least I know him, and I don't think I'm risking my life when I go to see him. I know that for all the things he's likely to do to me that will make me cry when I think about them in bed at night, he won't strangle me or stab me. In short, I'm already under his influence. He pays well.

At first, we kept in touch by e-mail. He became more insistent about arranging a new meeting, and I could sense his furious desire in the few lines he wrote me. He kept suggesting times to meet up, and I kept saying they weren't convenient. To pretend that I was trying, I'd offer him dates too, but at times when I knew he couldn't make it. I've often wondered why I play this game, why I haven't deleted him from my mailbox. I can't help it, I see him as a spare tire, someone who can help me out financially if I run out of money.

And right now, I need money since I want to go into exile, to flee far away, feeling that my life is leaning dangerously towards something I'll soon no longer be able to control. The main problem, of course, is money. I don't have a penny, not even to pay for my train ticket.

A friend of my mother's will put me up while I'm there, until I find a job and an apartment. I've managed to get a phoney medical certificate authorizing me to miss all my lectures at university. A college friend will take all my classes and I'll come and take my exams at the end of May. As for my job, too bad. I wasn't going to make a living in a telemarketing firm anyway. My entourage was warned of my imminent departure. My father sighed, preferring to ignore me rather than yell at me. He feels like he's reliving my senior year and my dropping out. But there's no way I'm giving up my studies, I'm continuing from a distance, university is my only way out. I'm so attached to this idea that I'm more motivated than ever to succeed.

In short, this exile is my last chance to free myself from the prostitution I'm losing myself in. As soon as I've got the money for this damn one-way ticket, I'll be off.

But I don't have the money. Ironically, I need to see Joe again to get away from my life as a prostitute. So I gave in to his proposals, and in an e-mail I asked him for his telephone number. After a few days' reflection, I called him.

- Joe, it's Laura.

- Hi, Laura, how are you?

I don't want to make small talk. So I cut the conversation short and go straight to the reason for my call.

- Five hours, Joe, not a minute more. Five hours at 1,000 euros.

He must have been surprised that I'd go straight to the heart of the matter, but he was quick to respond.

Deprivation

- Uh, that's fine, Laura. Five hours is perfect, and 1,000 euros is fine. Shall we meet as usual, in front of the hotel? Say Wednesday, 1pm?

- Yes, Wednesday's fine. I'll be there.

- Don't forget to bring sexy clothes.

I hung up immediately afterwards. Each time, he asks me to wear sexy, low-coverage clothes, because my jeans and T-shirts don't turn him on much, not enough. What he wants is a student playing grown-up in women's clothes. That's what he likes.

On Wednesday, we met in front of the hotel. He asked me to go in first. I can feel that he has a plan in mind, and I suppose there's a letter waiting for me on the bed, as usual.

Bingo, a note is indeed placed on the bed:

Hello, Laura

I'm really glad you agreed to come and I'm sure the meeting will be perfect.

As usual, I want you to take a shower first. Then come out of the room and knock on the door. When I answer, you come in.

These are the usual requests: the shower, the door, nothing new. In a way, that's reassuring. I put the letter down and headed for the bathroom.

So I head off to the shower and let the scalding water run slowly over my body. I feel limp and listless. I don't feel strong enough to fight back today.

After a thorough wash, I return to the bedroom. He's there, lying on the bed. Without a word, I continue to follow his instructions and leave the room. I knock, and still without giving him time to answer, panicking at the thought of running into someone in the corridor, I enter.

He doesn't move, doesn't speak, a sign that I must pick up where I left off.

Today we're going to stay in the room for about half an hour to talk, then we'll go to a place I want to show you, right next to the hotel.

A place? What place? Even if this hotel evokes disgusting moments, I know it. The places Joe might frequent outside this room are unknown to me, and therefore dangerous. Besides, I have no desire to be out in the open with him. I don't want to expose myself. My head is like a balance, where on the one hand my reason is screaming at me to go and on the other the 1,000 euros are glittering. This doesn't bode well.

It's a sex shop I know well, where we'll both have fun and enjoy ourselves.

I look up at him with questioning and somewhat frightened eyes.

- Come on, join me on the sofa," he says.

So that's what he calls "talking". He's going to pull out all his rhetoric to convince me to come with him to this creepy place, I can already see the picture.

- Listen, this is a great place, and I'm really excited about it. It's a stone's throw from the hotel, so there's no risk of anyone seeing us on the way, it's really close.

Deprivation

- Joe, I'm not feeling it at all, there will be people there, and I don't want to be seen. I'm not reassured. No, really, I don't feel like it at all, I'd rather stay here.

- But no, Laura, don't worry. It's safe there, there'll be no worries, I can assure you. No one will see you. There's a room at the back of the store where only the regulars go. It's a very dark place, no one will see us there, you can trust me. There are videos we can watch together, it's very exciting. I've been there regularly with women and it's always gone well.

He knows to be careful with me, that I'll refuse. I'm obviously not familiar with places like this, and the only image I have of them is a gloomy one. I can't imagine what awaits me, and that's the problem. After several minutes, he finally says:

- Look, let's go and then we'll see. If you really don't feel comfortable, we'll come back to the hotel. You know, I understand completely, I'm a very shy person and very modest too.

I sighed, but a voice whispered to me: *"1,000 euros, Laura, and then you're out of here. You leave all this shit behind. Without that money, you'll never leave."*

- Very well, then. But as soon as I want, we'll go home," I finally say.

So we set off for the sex shop. It's just around the corner from the hotel.

As we enter, the doorbell rings. I face the store cashier. He's between 25 and 30 years old and so handsome that I freeze in front of him for a moment. What a guy! On the street, in other circumstances, I might have gone to ask him for his phone number. But here, in this place, accompanied by Joe who could have been my father, I'm blushing all the way to my ears.

He noticed me too. For a second, I saw in his eyes that he liked me, but that look suddenly turned to disgust. He's judging me, probably thinking I'm just some whore who comes to sex shops to get fucked. He certainly blames himself for finding me to his liking for a moment. I'm a strong-tempered person who never lets things get me down, but I must admit I feel lower than dirt. This guy reflects back to me everything I refuse to see: the image of Laura in her second life, the image of Laura the prostitute who is kept by old men. Yes, in his eyes, I'm just a whore. But then, he's a sex-shop cashier!

Joe pays the entrance fee, a paltry few euros. He moves quickly to the back room, hidden by large black curtains. More curtains. They're there every time I meet a customer. They confirm that what I'm doing is wrong, is dirty. I slip inside the room, avoiding the gaze of the salesman, who is no longer looking at me anyway.

The place is very dark, and it takes me a few seconds to get used to the darkness. All I can smell at first is something wild, the scent of human flesh. A shiver runs through my body. When I can finally make out my surroundings, I see a large overhead projector in front of me, showing a porn movie of a vulgar blonde screaming with pleasure. About twenty chairs are set up in rows in front of the screen. At first glance, there are just over ten people in the room, all men, slumped over in the chairs, or standing and masturbating. I restrain myself from groaning in disgust. The room is rather large, from what I can see, all decorated in black. The whole thing looks a bit like a nightclub: you can tell the place has been worked on to give the impression of a trendy venue. The result is not good: you know very well when you enter this place that something fishy is going on.

- Here, pull up a chair," says Joe, "and we'll watch the movie together.

Lost, I don't know what to do. Sitting next to these guys means giving them a chance to see who I am. What if I know one of them? I don't have a passable justification. Being in a sex shop choosing a video is fine, you get a reputation for being a bit of a naughty girl. Being in this room leaves no alibi.

Like a 6-year-old girl, I listen to the orders of my paternalistic representative. I take a seat in the second row, after studying the available seats that don't put me too close to the other men. Joe, on the other hand, stands back and observes. He looks at the sex-shop customers while glancing at the film. I can feel all eyes on me. I'm the only woman in the place. The customers must be thinking how lucky they are today: they might be able to realize their fantasies with a real woman.

I try to watch the film and think of nothing, but it's simply impossible. The screams of a blonde on the screen, the moans of pleasure from the guys, I can't ignore all these noises. I don't want to close my eyes. As much as possible in a situation like this, I want to remain in control of myself.

Joe approaches me and says, pointing to a man in his fifties:

- This one, you can let him approach you. I told him about you, he won't do anything to you, I know him. This one's legit too.

This time he's talking about another guy of the same age, who's in the front row. He points at them with impunity, they're far too busy with their video anyway. So he knows them all, and worse, he's telling them about me! I feel a horrible trap closing in on me. I've been relying on Joe to protect me, when he's the one responsible for my presence here. I murmur a little "OK", while continuing to observe my surroundings, as if to spot where the danger will come from first.

- That's enough, we've looked at enough pictures for today.

Joe said this as if he were pulling me away from an activity I'd been enjoying. In an absolute sense, and given the situation, I'd undoubtedly have preferred to stay for five hours watching this sex movie. I know that when I get up and follow him, the serious stuff will start. I tremble in anticipation.

- Did you bring your things?" he asks.

- Yes," I say, pointing to a plastic bag that I got rid of as soon as I arrived by placing it against a wall.

- Well, go and change now, you can use one of those cabins over there.

He points to a booth I didn't notice behind me. There are three identical ones lined up against the wall opposite the mini-cinema.

I grab my clothes and enter the cabin. There's room for only one person, and the only object inside is a commonplace chair. The white light blinds me a little as I enter, after the near-darkness of the room. I pull a low-cut black nightie from my bag. I change quickly, fearing that someone will enter the cabin and try to touch me. When I raise my head, I see that the cabin is dotted with holes at different heights, but I don't immediately understand their purpose.

When I emerge, arms crossed over my cleavage to try and hide a little of my skin, Joe is waiting for me outside. He's a little impressed by my get-up; I don't usually make much effort to bring sexy clothes.

- Very nice, very nice nightie! Now listen, you're going to go back into that cabin and wait a bit. When they approach, you're going to do what you want.

What do you mean "they"? I don't understand what he's saying. I don't have time to figure it out. Joe gently pushes me inside the cabin, and closes the door behind me. I sit in the chair, unsure. The next thing I know, sex is being inserted into a hole. So that's what they're for… They're all going to come, waiting for me to touch them and more. But where have I fallen? I feel naive to have believed that everything would pass quickly.

I hear moans of pleasure outside. I jerk back and immediately turn the cabin latch to lock myself in. Throwing myself back, I feel something against my shoulder. Another sex. Then a third, then more. Even if I'd wanted to, I couldn't have touched them all, there are so many.

I suddenly feel nauseous in front of this absurd picture. I take my head in my hands and curl up so that I can no longer see or feel them. I'm nothing, no more than an object, a mere masturbation machine. This is a nightmare, this can't really be happening. If this is the price of going to Paris, I don't want it anymore, I want to go home now.

I raise my head to the top of the cabin. I see a man's eye watching me. I understand the perversity of this device. I turn my head away from the piercing eye. My gaze meets another.

They're all watching me, clamoring, impatient with desire, to feel my hands or my mouth.

I lower my face and wait, hands against my ears, shutting out the world. I scream inwardly. I murmur a song in my head, to stop hearing their moans. I'm on the verge of a nervous breakdown. I don't cry, I've reached a stage of inner pain so deep it won't allow any more tears.

I don't know how long I spend like this, my head buried in my knees, but when I lift it, the sexes are gone. I turn around frantically to check. This situation is awful. How long have I been moaning? Ten minutes? An hour? I'm totally unable to give even an estimate.

Now I've got to get out of this hellish place, but I'm afraid the perverts are waiting for me outside and will pounce on me. At the same time, I can't stay in this cabin forever. After a moment's hesitation, I carefully turn the latch.

To my great relief, no one is waiting for me at the exit except Joe. He's wearing a delighted smile, probably one of the eyes that have been happily checking me out in the cabin.

- So, what did you think?

I don't answer: he knows very well what I thought. I'm freezing, shivering with fear. The most absurd part of this story is undeniably that I depend entirely on him. There's no doubt that it was he who asked them to stop. His gaze betrays a feeling of absolute power. Something in his eyes gives me a glimpse of what's to come. If I don't react right away, I'll probably get caught by all these men. So, driven by the energy of desperation, I grab my things and run. Joe and the other men look at me dejectedly. He tries to talk to

Deprivation

me, but I can't hear anything. I barely have time to get out of the sex shop half-naked, my things in my arms. Joe is already behind me.

- Calm down, Laura. I'll give you 500 euros anyway.

I walk, losing my balance. I feel like I'm going to faint. I feel drugged, drunk, I can't stand up, my legs can't carry me. But I still have enough survival instinct to grab the envelope.

We return to the hotel in silence. I can still smell the men on my body. We make our way without a word. If I speak, I'll slap Joe or spit in his face. I hate myself for not realizing he was just a vicious old fool. I want to end it, forever. All I can think about now is taking my money and getting far, far away. I feel so dirty, I want to cry, but I can't anymore.

Once in the room, I said:

- I'm not staying. Give me my money now.

- Go take your shower, I'll leave the envelope on the bed. See you Thursday, what do you think?

After what he's just put me through, does he really think I'd agree to see him again on Thursday? Even if the 500 euros isn't enough to get me to Paris, I never want to see him again. It's out of the question to plan another meeting with such a rotter. Better not tell him, we're alone in the room and now that I know he has no limits, I don't want to provoke him. He's still in a position to hit me.

- Yes, we'll see you on Thursday.

I have to take a shower, I can't stand the smell any longer. Alone in the bathroom, I forbid myself to sit on the floor, otherwise I'd never get up again. I hear the door slam, Joe's gone. After fifteen minutes of scrubbing my skin and hair like a maniac, under scalding water, I put my clothes back on and leave the bathroom.

An envelope is waiting for me on the bed, as agreed. I open it, enticed by the money I'm counting on to console me, if only for a second, for my misfortune.

It contains 100 euros. I check: only 100 euros. It's missing 400. He's ripped me off. Tears well up and my sobbing ends in a howl. I reach for my phone like a fury and dial his number so fast, my vision clouded by tears, that I make a mistake and have to dial three times, which drives me even crazier. My hands are shaking, I'm screaming wildly as I bang my little fist against the wall. His mobile doesn't answer. He's probably long gone by now.

I shake the envelope downwards, still hoping to find what's due me. I find nothing. I even move the desk, shaking the sheets violently. I look around as if haggard, trying to convince myself that he must have left the rest of my money somewhere in this dreadful room. Nothing, definitely. Instead, there's a letter on the bed, which he must have placed under the envelope when he left.

It was scribbled in a hurry, probably while I was taking a shower.

Laura, as you can see, there's only 100 euros in the envelope, instead of the 500 euros planned. I'll give you the rest on Thursday, when we meet. I just wanted to make sure I saw you again before you left for Paris. Trust me, you'll get your money. Have a good day, Laura.

I throw the letter on the floor in a rage. Gone Paris, gone the new life, I'll have to stay here. I'll never get out, my life is stuck in prostitution forever.

The roles have now reversed. Today, I'm the one who's being taken advantage of.

Chapter 21

Escape

April 2, 2007

It's Thursday and I'm back in front of the hotel, not believing it. Of course, Joe hasn't shown up. My anger hasn't subsided, and after half an hour I'm already stamping my feet and cursing at him alone in the street. Passers-by turn around, but I don't notice them; I've only got one thing on my mind at the moment: getting my money back.

When I got home, I left him an explosive message on his unanswered phone, shouting that he'd better call me back and give me my money. Radio silence for three days. Three days I spend moping about my fate, crying whenever I think of Paris. I see the Eiffel Tower in a blur, and all my beautiful projects falling apart.

Three days later, my phone rang:

- Laura?

I recognize his voice immediately. My blood runs cold.

- Goddamn it, Joe, you've made a fool out of me, and I want my money now!

I scream into the machine. Fortunately, I'm home alone.

- I know, Laura, I know. Wait, let me explain…

- Explain what? You're an asshole, you're going to give me my money back right now!

- Laura, I'm not at home right now. I've had a heart attack and I'm convalescing in the South of France, near Perpignan.

I stop my stream of insults for a second.

- I wanted to transfer money to you, but my wife blocked my accounts. I think she suspects something.

The old Laura would have believed it without hesitation. The new Laura, who was born the day she was duped, no longer lets herself be fooled by these lies.

- I don't believe you, Joe, it's not working. Give me back my money.

- Laura, I'm telling you the truth, I'm very sick, I have cancer. I won't live long.

This sentence makes my blood run cold. I have to admit that I felt sad when I heard the news, despite everything he had done to me. The feeling doesn't last more than a second though, I hate him again. He continues:

- Listen, Laura, I'm leaving this place tomorrow. We've got to meet again, so I can give you your money back. I'll give it back, I promise. Besides, I really want to see you again.

I hang up. I don't believe it anymore. I'll never believe it again.

Chapter 22

Break-in

April 17, 2007

Two weeks after the Joe episode, I'm back home with my arms full of groceries. For once, I'm tired of depriving myself. There's another reason. I'm hosting a friend in my apartment and we've decided to have a meal fit for kings: tandoori chicken and wild rice. The last thing I want is for him to realize that I have nothing in my cupboards. We're in for a treat and my lips are quivering with anticipation. I'm in a very good mood and I resist the weight of the plastic bags by humming.

Arriving home, I clear away the victuals in the kitchen and hurry to my temporary flatmate. As I prepare dinner, he says to me:

- Someone tried to reach you half an hour ago on the landline. I told him to call back later.

- Did he say who he was?

- No. I mean, he said he was an old friend. Apparently, he hadn't heard from you in a while, so he wanted to know how you were.

- Well, if it's important, he'll call back.

An hour later, in the middle of dinner, the phone rings again. I get up to answer it. I immediately recognize his voice. Pierre. The soft contractor. The James Bond in slippers.

- Laura, it's Pierre.

- How did you get my number? I said curtly.

It all comes back to me at once: the snack, the cigarette I smoked, my bag open and free to access. I don't try to find out more, to understand why he waited so long to call me: the result is there, he has my landline number, which implies he also has my address. Panic makes me nervous, and the first sounds out of my mouth sound threatening:

- Don't you ever call me on this number again, you hear me?

- Yes, but it's your fault. You say you'll get back to me and you don't! I want to see you again, Laura!

This guy is crazy and it's obvious now that I've been obsessing over him all these months. I'm totally freaking out, this man could be downstairs right now talking to me, he could be calling me from my street, my building…

- Look, it's simple: if you don't leave me alone, I'll call your work and tell them how you're screwing 19-year-old prostitutes! Call me back and I'll ruin your life.

The threat has paid off. A silence falls between us. I hang up before he can get a word in.

The next few days are spent in perpetual fear of finding him downstairs when I go out. I constantly look back at the people in the street, convinced I've spotted him among the passers-by. I know he hasn't given up, because every time I check my answering machine, the robot voice tells me how many times he's called, e.g. "This caller tried to reach you 26 times today without leaving a message." 26 times! What a freak! After hearing my answering machine tell me for the umpteenth time that Pierrot le fou has shown up again, I decide to call the last number calling. I get a girl who tells me that Pierre Machintruc isn't in and that I should call back tomorrow morning. I understand that he makes all his calls to me from work, and now that I know his surname, I'm determined to give him a hard time. Stupid of him. I'm sure he thinks I wouldn't dare mess with him.

The next day, I quietly dial the number, I have a plan. I get straight through to him. I can feel his face decompose at the sound of my voice.

- Listen to me, Pierre. I just wanted to warn you that if you ever, ever try to contact me again, I'll call the cops right away.

- Why would you do such a thing?

- Because when you got my name, you should have made sure I wasn't underage.

He gasps for breath. I hear him utter a little "shit". He begins to stammer, in a bantering tone:

- I'm sorry, Laura, but I just wanted to see you again…

I'm at my wits' end. I've been swindled out of a huge amount of money by Joe, my move to Paris is in serious jeopardy, and I don't need some apathetic businessman to piss me off on top of it all. I start screaming into the phone, venting all my hatred on him:

- I'm going to file a complaint against you for harassment! I know your address, your phone number, everything about you and I'm going to use it if you ever come near me again!

- But you're a whore, Laura.

The bastard. He had it coming, threats apparently weren't enough. I decide to put my plan into action.

- So you don't know they're protected by the cops?" I say in a snide voice.

Not true in the case of student prostitutes, but who cares, Pierre is far too scared to go and check.

- So never again do you hear me, never again do you phone me or write me e-mails, you're out of my life the way you came in: in two seconds!

I hang up on him. I don't need to wait for his approval to end the conversation. I know I've got rid of him. I've made up my mind: money or no money, I'm making a promise to myself to get out of this town as soon as possible.

Chapter 23

Exile

April 19, 2007

I can't stand still in front of my Spanish text. It's 5 p.m., and this is the last class I'm attending at the University of V. Last night, I picked up my train tickets for Paris. I'm leaving tomorrow on the 12:47 train, arriving in the capital two hours later.

Looking at my copy, I have an overwhelming urge to cry. I can't believe that tonight it will all be over. In an hour's time, I'll be nothing but a runaway student. No matter how many times I tell myself that, as things stand, I have no choice, that my departure for Paris is essential, I see this abandonment as a failure. Once again, I haven't finished my year of study, it seems to me that my destiny is catching up with me, that I'm not cut out to sit in a classroom and listen to a teacher. And yet, in this case, things have nothing to do with my final year, but I can't help feeling like a coward for having to leave.

The tickets were expensive, as I don't have a discount card, but if that's the price I have to pay to be safe, I'm ready to break my piggy bank. The hardest thing to bear is giving up university. I just can't bring myself to do it. I love this student life, I love going to college every day and learning. Even though I've had to do everything I've done, I've always felt at home on campus. But I'm not giving up on my studies. I'm determined to finish this year whatever the cost, attendance or not. I've given too much of myself this year to just throw it all away at the last minute. All these clients, all these problems, were all about continuing to study, not giving up.

So I had to find someone serious and trustworthy to mail me the courses. A friend from college immediately came to mind. I don't know her very well, we're just classmates. We naturally sit next to each other for almost every class, and we get on pretty well, even though I've never seen her outside university. I had to invent a lame excuse to explain my departure to her, a family affair. It seemed the most plausible. I was embarrassed to lie to him, but then again, I couldn't do otherwise. In exchange for a cash advance for postage and photocopying, she agreed to send me the courses.

Classwork doesn't count towards the final result, and with my medical certificate, the teachers can't blame me for my absences from tutorials. Even though I know I'm not really giving up college, I'm sad. The little world I dreamed of in September has collapsed. I feel like crying because I feel like the victim of an injustice; I feel like crying because my hopes have been dashed. I'm going to continue with distance learning, but will I be able to do it? Am I strong enough, disciplined enough?

I handed in my resignation at work yesterday. Again, I felt a twinge of sadness, not because I was giving up a job I enjoyed - on the contrary - but because it was an escape. It allowed me to get out of the house, immerse myself in my work and stop thinking about my life. On the whole, I got on well with my colleagues, and they often helped me when I didn't know how to do something. My boss didn't really question why I was leaving. He must see dozens of students coming and going every year, so it was nothing out of the ordinary.

I don't know what to expect in Paris. Maybe nothing will be better, maybe I won't even last a fortnight on my own there. I know that at the beginning, it's going to be a real struggle all over again. I'll have to run around looking for work. I'll also have to get used to living with someone again, especially someone I don't know very well. And above all, I won't have anyone to help me, support me, console me if one day I don't feel up to it. I'm ready to face all that, because it will be with a view to a healthy future, something better. Prostitution, on the other hand, has only offered me the worst.

I've told my mother's friend who's supposed to put me up, but she can't pick me up at the station. As she lives in the suburbs, she told me which RER to take to get to her house. Of course, this is only temporary, she's just helping me out. I've got to find another place to live quickly, anything from a flat-share to a maid's room. Even though I'm completely demoralized, I have the feeling that nothing will be as hard as what I've been through here in V.

In front of my copy, I don't listen to the lecture. I should be enjoying my last few hours in this majestic lecture hall, but my head is full of dark thoughts. I'm thinking about tonight, about the suitcases I'll have to pack on my own. The courses and books I'll have to take with me to keep studying. I'm so attached to them that I wouldn't leave them behind for the world, even if my suitcase weighs a ton. Clothes aren't that important either - I've done without shopping this year. Since September, more than ever, I've had to learn to prioritize things.

I'm keeping my apartment until the end of the month, since I've paid the rent. It'll be empty, but never mind. My father will come later with a friend to collect the furniture. I also told my landlady I was leaving, which obviously didn't make her very happy, but I assured her I'd find her another tenant very quickly. She's never liked me, and I can understand her, I've often been late with my payments, despite my best efforts. I've advertised at the university for a vacant studio. In V., that shouldn't be difficult, even at this time of year. Basically, I don't care. I've got a lot of other things on my mind right now.

There are only ten minutes left in the class. People are already getting restless, anxious to get home. I'd like to hang on to my seat and not have to leave. They can't understand. Not for a second can they imagine what I've had to do this year to fend off my constant troubles. The general hubbub drowns out the voice of the teacher, who, resigned, decides to end the class. After a certain hour, he must realize that the students' brains are becoming hermetically sealed to all knowledge, and that they need to get some fresh air.

People jump to their feet as soon as they hear the teacher say "see you next week". I myself, carried along by a certain habit, carelessly toss my course sheets into my bag. Then I get up slowly, put on my jacket and leave the lecture hall, as if it were an ordinary day.

Outside, I embrace my college friend who's in charge of sending me her lessons. She wishes me luck with a touch of compassion in her eyes. I lied to her about why I left, but I'm entitled to her compassion just the same.

Deep down, I tell myself I'm not such a coward for leaving. On the contrary, it's a wise decision, as I'm risking too much by staying in V. from now on. I don't really belong here anymore. If I stay, I'll never get out. If I leave, I have a chance to rebuild my life. Here, everything has become impossible.

I wink at my girlfriend and head for the metro, as if after a normal day at school.

Chapter 24

The Beginning

April 24, 2007

It's incredibly hot in Paris for April. I packed my suitcase in a panic, I couldn't take all my light clothes. I don't really care. It's hot and I've achieved my goal of leaving V.

It's back to the way I planned it. My two goals are to find a job first and then, once I've stabilized, an apartment. I give myself two weeks to get a job, anything. After that, I'll have to accept my failure and return to V. I can't take advantage of my mother's friend Sandra's hospitality.

The mere thought of having to go back to V. makes my blood run cold and doubly motivates me to find something as quickly as possible. For the past week, I've been going non-stop. Armed with my CV, I've been scouring restaurants and adverts to find work as quickly as possible. I didn't want to give that horrible solution time to re-emerge in my mind. So far, I've been strong, buoyed by the immense hope that Paris is my land of exile, where no one knows me as a prostitute, where I can start afresh and begin a new life.

The flat-sharing arrangement with my mother's friend Sandra is going well so far. She welcomed me with open arms, happy to have some company in her apartment. At one time, she was very close to my mother, so she was delighted to get to know her daughter. Now in her fifties, this woman wears the sufferings of her life on her face. She works all day as an accountant for a household appliance company and hates her job. She often comes home tired, worn out by her colleagues and the mountains of figures she's had to line up all day. I think she's pretty, though, especially when she comes home from work and puts her dyed-blond hair up in a bun. She lives a quiet little life, lacking nothing but far from being rich. There's nothing luxurious about her apartment, the furniture is mostly salvaged, but she's managed to make the place pleasant, with fabrics in warm colors.

We often have dinner together and she even helps me write cover letters to find a job. One evening, she confided in me that she had struggled like me during her first years after university. I wondered if she'd ever considered prostitution as a recourse. Strangely enough, if she had, I'd find a certain comfort in it, as it would make me feel I wasn't all alone.

I feel at home with her, even if I miss my little independent life in my own apartment. She's set up her living room to receive me, unfolding the sofa bed. Every morning, I politely put it back in place, wanting to disturb as little as possible.

Since my arrival, I haven't really been able to concentrate on my apartment search. As I don't have a job, I can't guarantee that I'll be able to put together a file, as that would be a waste of time. I prefer to take things in their own time, aware that

I don't have much. In spite of everything, Sandra's kindness urges me not to stay too long. I know from experience that relationships between two people unravel more quickly than you'd think in situations like this, where one owes something to the other. I'm already so uncomfortable with having to depend on someone that there's no way I'm going to make her uncomfortable with my presence too.

Anguish returns. Alone in Paris, far from family and friends, I have no support. I need to make a decision quickly: return to V. and admit my failure, or take action here in Paris. I choose action. The idea of having to return to V. paralyzes me. I've seen much worse in my life, I can hold on.

As of today, no one has called me back for a job. It's been a week now and I'm starting to panic. My pockets are empty and I'm not sure I'll make it through the week with the little money I've managed to bring in.

I'm also caught up in my past. Joe keeps harassing me. He leaves me daily messages begging me to come back to V., saying he's offering me the train ticket. He claims he needs to see me again before he dies. His rates are so exorbitant as to be improbable. I screen all his calls and bypass all his vices: if my phone rings without displaying a number, I simply don't answer. I have to admit that more than once, I've been tempted to drop everything and go back to smelling the money.

In my need to come to terms with my past, I realize more and more that I can't do it without talking about it. At night, I can't fall asleep. I toss and turn in bed, images of horror flash before my eyes. I often cry, realizing that I'll have to deal with this experience for the rest of my life. Talk, yes, but to whom? I scour the discussion forums devoted to student prostitution, without ever finding the answers to my questions. On the contrary, some of the girls who frequent these sites castigate me for daring to put forward the idea that prostitution is a real scourge among students. They talk such nonsense, so far removed from what I've ever felt, that I soon don't even log on any more, denying that this channel has the power to help me liberate myself psychologically.

When I can't sleep, I find refuge only in my writing and my studies. My evenings and nights, when all is silent, I devote them to telling my story, my emotions. I write for hours on end, thinking of nothing else. Little by little, I realize that I'm exorcising all the malaise that's eating away at me from the inside. The more I type on my computer keyboard, the one Joe gave me, the more I gain perspective on my life. I'm beginning to feel a glimmer of hope that I'll get out of this one day. Maybe I won't be a whore anymore.

I'm also working harder than ever on my courses, even more than when I was in the lecture theaters at V. I don't want to ruin everything, my future seems so uncertain. This week, I received the first classes in the mail, which filled me with joy. My college girlfriend hasn't forgotten me. I'm holding out hope as best I can: if I manage to find a good job in Paris, I'll put some money aside and enroll here at the university. I'm sure I can do it. My tumultuous life has given me rage, I know what the galère is and I don't want to fall back into it. Sometimes, too, I cry when faced with an exercise or a text I don't understand. I tell myself that my father is right, that I've never done things right. Maybe not, but I did what I could with what I had, almost nothing. You can blame me, you can judge me, but I can't go back. On the contrary, I've only ever lived for my future, I've only ever prostituted myself to be able to continue studying. You can blame me, yes, but I've never given up.

Today, I don't allow myself to be depressed, I have too many things to do and to undertake. Too many things to achieve.

Chapter 25

Dependency

June 17, 2007

The last month in Paris was intense. My job search paid off after two weeks, right on target. I finally landed a job as a waitress in a chic restaurant in the center of Paris. I'm still living with Sandra and the commute to and from her apartment is exhausting, but at least I'm earning money. On the metro, taking advantage of the long journey, I read the lessons I put in my bag before leaving in the morning. I force myself to stay focused despite my eyes closing on their own. My timetable isn't stable and sometimes I finish late at night, when there's no subway. The first time, I took a cab. I didn't really have a choice, as I don't know my colleagues very well, and I couldn't see myself asking them to put me up. When I saw the amount on the meter, I promised myself I'd never do it again. I couldn't possibly spend all the money I earn on cabs to get home.

Once again, I'm faced with a vicious circle: yes, I have a job, but I won't soon be able to keep it if I can't keep the evening shifts. So I'm scouring the classified ads looking for a place to live. I thought I'd seen the worst of V. in terms of prices, but Paris is hell. I can't find anything within my meager price range, not even a maid's room. Shared flats are sometimes more affordable, but they ask for a lot of guarantees, sometimes even more than for an apartment. I suppose landlords have to put more pressure on tenants to pay on time: as the number of tenants increases, the risk of not seeing the money is multiplied.

At first, Sandra kept telling me, "But don't worry, you can stay as long as you like, you're not bothering me at all!" Faced with the obvious need to live close to my place of work, she began to help in any way she could. She asked around to see if anyone had a spare room. Nothing, not even a cage where I could take refuge.

Her kindness gradually turned into mere politeness. Seeing that my apartment search was going nowhere, she began to distance herself more and more from me, which is only human. We no longer have meals together, and she only speaks to me vaguely. As expected, my presence is beginning to weigh on her. I can feel that I'm disturbing her daily routine. Her apartment isn't very big, and the fact that I occupy the living room doesn't help matters.

One evening, as usual, I come home from work very late. I'm exhausted and just want to go to bed right away. I find her in the living room with two friends, chatting over a glass of wine after dinner. At the sight of me, Sandra makes a sort of grimace that says it all: she wishes I wasn't here, so she could enjoy her friends in peace. I feel sorry for her and try to make myself look small, rushing into the bathroom to take a shower. When I come out, her friends have already left.

- Are your friends home?

- Yes, we couldn't go on talking in the living room since that's where you sleep.

I've gone beyond the limit of what she can bear. Without a word, I lie down after unfolding the sofa. I know I'll have to leave tomorrow, before Sandra kicks me out in exasperation.

At work, I ask a colleague who has a large apartment in Paris if she can put me up. We get on well and I know she won't refuse. I hate situations like that.

- Not for long, just long enough to find something suitable.

She accepts, with a smile on her face. It's often like that at first: people say yes, happy not to be alone in their own home, but after a while they realize they'd rather be on their own. What's more, in Paris, where apartments are often very small, people quickly step on each other's toes. I know that this solution is only temporary and that I'll have to find another one quickly. For her, but also for me. I can't, I don't want to depend on others anymore.

I pack my bags that evening when I get home. Sandra hugs me, surprised by my quick decision. She's certainly saddened by my situation too, and perhaps feels guilty. But I know that once I'm gone, she'll do what she hasn't been able to do for a month: sprawl out on the sofa and enjoy her solitude all over again.

My repeated troubles often bring me back to my dark thoughts. What if I dropped everything? What if I accepted Joe's proposal? I'd be out of this mess. I know that deep down, this solution isn't a solution at all, it's only temporary. It shines with all the money it can offer, but when you get closer, it becomes dirty and dangerous.

I call my college friend, who sends me the courses, to give her my new address. Once again, she doesn't try to understand. Good, because I can't come up with another lie. She's in the middle of revision and starting to panic with exams looming.

- Laura, you're going home for your exams, aren't you? If you like, I could put you up.

I say yes, of course, thanking her for the offer, which I'm going to have to accept, since I have nowhere to go during the week of midterms in May.

So I have to negotiate with my boss at the restaurant, working twelve hours a day for two weeks to make up for the week I'm away. With all my overtime, I can take five days off. That's exactly what I need to pass my exams.

I tell my mother I'll be back, but that I won't have time to visit her and my father. She's obviously very disappointed, but deep down I know she's proud of her daughter, who never gives up and takes responsibility.

The week of midterms is drawing to a close. All I want to do is curl up in bed and fall asleep for hours, not having to worry about it anymore. Still, I don't stop, working late into the night with my friend. We motivate each other. The human body is malleable, and the knowledge that my university year will soon be over keeps me from getting tired. I want so much to succeed this year, it would have been unfair not to, after all I've been through. I've studied too hard, revised too much to collapse at the last minute.

My Great Education

I won't let myself. I've given everything this year, even my own body. Failure is out of the question.

At the end of the mid-term exams, I jumped on a train to Paris, having warmly thanked my friend for her welcome and support. She didn't ask me any questions, surely considering that my private life was my own business.

I get right back to work, still at a frantic pace. I don't even have time to think about the results, the papers I've handed in. I've done as much as I can, now I just have to wait.

A few days later, in front of my computer, I wait for the results to appear. I've had this date in mind for two weeks. I type in my student number, which will tell me my results in a few seconds. I'm trembling, stressed. What if I've failed? Perhaps I've failed to convince in my essays. My tiredness and frustration may have shown in the lines I wrote…

The result suddenly appeared. I passed, with honors. In front of my computer screen, I weep with joy. So all the hardship I'd been through this year hadn't been in vain after all.

Chapter 26

Hope

September 5, 2007

I've passed my exams and I'm still in Paris. I'm 19 and a new year is beginning. I've continued to work in the restaurant all summer, trying to save as much money as I can. I'm still living with my colleague and, contrary to what I thought, things are going rather well. I give her all I can for the rent, which relieves her a little for her expenses. Our roommate situation is nothing like the one I had with Manu. She's having a hard time too, but she understands me.

I communicate a lot with my parents by phone: our relationship has evolved a lot. I must have grown up faster than anyone else last year, and it shows in my behavior. I can feel them supporting me. I know from my mother that my father was impressed by my exam success and my courage. They never understood why I left and I hope they never will. I also know that they regret that they still can't help me financially, but their moral encouragement spurs me on. They're proving to me today what I've always known: that they'll always be there, despite my choices.

However, I'm still looking for accommodation. I'm going to enroll in my second year of university in Paris and I need to work in decent conditions. I don't want to go back to V. I know it's a foregone conclusion. Nor do I want to take advantage of my colleague's kindness any longer. The restaurant has offered me a part-time permanent contract, which I'm going to accept. With this salary guarantee, I suppose things should be easier.

But it turns out to be harder than expected. From studio visits to maid's room visits, I realized that my application was no match for the others. I don't have a guarantor, and even with a permanent contract, landlords prefer to entrust the keys to an apartment to a young person who will have someone behind him in case of need. Which I don't have. I hear my parents don't earn enough. No kidding.

So my future remains uncertain. My head is full of dreams, but society constantly brings me back to reality. I want to continue my studies, I want to continue learning, but the obstacles are always there. Will I be able to find an apartment? Will I be able to alternate work and study? But above all, will I be strong enough not to fall back into prostitution? The money in sex is too fast, too important, for me not to think about it. I know what I want, but I also know that it's not always in line with reality. High hopes but low means.

Afterword by Eva Clouet[1]

Student Prostitution
in the Age of the Internet

"In France, nearly 40,000 students are said to prostitute themselves in order to pursue their studies. This information, revealed by the SUD-Étudiant union in the spring of 2006 during the movement against the "equal opportunities" law, aims to draw the French government's attention to the "student reality". In its demands, this student union highlights the difficult living conditions currently experienced by a number of students (scarcity and high cost of housing, very tight month-ends, difficulty in combining salaried work and university work, etc.), and points the finger at the contradictions in the responses proposed by the public authorities to alleviate these dysfunctions.

---

1. Eva Clouet is 23 years old and studying for a Master 2 in Sociology - "Gender and Social Policies".

From autumn 2006 onwards, the media (mainly the press and television) seized on the news, highlighting the problem of students' economic insecurity from a new, racy angle. In the run-up to an election campaign, the "40,000" figure sounded like a bombshell. Curiosity, surprise, indignation, incomprehension, skepticism, fantasy… the subject of student prostitution has entered the public arena, provoking debate and reaction.

In our societies, prostitution - whatever its form - remains a highly stigmatized practice, and the image of the[2] prostitute remains, in the collective imagination, often associated with a person "on the margins" because "so desperate as to sell her body". So when it comes to students, the unease is even greater. The image we have of the prostitute - a foreign woman waiting for a customer on the sidewalk[3] - seems incompatible with the images we have of our students. And yet, as Laura testifies, student prostitution is a reality in our country. So

---

2. By convention, we'll use the term "prostitute" to refer to men, women and transgender people who offer sexual services in exchange for payment.

3. In February 2006, 138 second-year psychology and medicine students from the Nantes university campus were questioned on the themes of non-student and student prostitution. The results of this survey show that, according to this sample, the "typical profile" of a prostitute in France corresponds to "a young person (84.8% of respondents), female (97.8%), foreign (82.6%), soliciting on the street (71.3%)". This "profile" echoes that conveyed on a fairly regular basis in the media - when they talk about prostitution networks in particular - while emphasizing the most visible form of prostitution (that involving street soliciting). However, according to the work of the "prostitution mission" of the Médecins du Monde association (Nantes branch), street prostitution in France accounts for only 40% of all prostitution.

how is it that, in France, a world power whose education system - however criticized and criticizable - is often held up as an example, some students prostitute themselves?

While to date no serious study has been able to put a figure on the extent of the phenomenon - in fact, the figure of "40,000" is not based on any scientific work and is therefore an estimate - Laura's story and my study of the world of student escorts highlight a number of elements, offering some keys to understanding the vast issue of student prostitution.

1. STUDENT PROSTITUTION: A HETEROGENEOUS REALITY

Today, there are as many prostitutes[4], as there are places of prostitution, and as many ways of prostituting oneself. In this context, anthropologist and political scientist Janine Mossuz-Lavau explains that it now seems more appropriate to speak of "prostitutions" (in the plural) rather than "prostitution", "given the diversity of situations[5]". Each location (studios, bars, clubs, Internet, massage parlors, highway rest areas, woods, vans, etc.) has its own prostitution reality, with its own actors, its own codes, its own specificities, its own rates, its own clientele, its own constraints and its own stakes. Student prostitutes are no exception to this diversity. While

---

4. Individuals belonging to a social category recognized as such; for example: students, middle-class young people, etc.
5. Janine Mossuz-Lavau and Marie-Élisabeth Handman, *La Prostitution à Paris*, Paris, Éditions de la Martinière, 2005, p. 13.

some students choose the street as their place of prostitution[6], others solicit on campus or through "classified ads" and receive their clients in their dormitory, still others prostitute themselves in the alcoves of the famous "hostess bars" (or "cork bars") or "massage parlors", and others - like Laura - use the Internet to monetize their sexual services. Student prostitution is therefore not a homogeneous reality, since it covers a diversity of forms and practices.

However, the democratization of access to new means of communication such as Minitel in the 1980s, and the Internet and mobile telephony today, seems to have intensified the development of "amateur" prostitution (as opposed to "professional" prostitution) and "occasional" prostitution, in which the student category has a certain visibility.

Among the many faces of student prostitution, this afterword aims to shed some light on a particular form of prostitution - the very one practiced by Laura - namely voluntary (chosen) prostitution, carried out independently (without a pimp) and occasionally by students via the Internet.

The Internet and the figure of the student "escort girl"

When it comes to prostitution, the Minitel of the 1980s, with its famous "pink messaging services", and now the Internet offer significant advantages, both for customers (demand) and for those wishing to prostitute themselves

---

6. On this subject, see the testimony of Sélénia, a student who prostituted herself for a year on the streets of Toulouse, *in* E. Philippe, "Étudiante, je me suis prostituée", *Esprit Femme* (mensuel), February 2007, n° 21, p. 56-57.

(supply). In addition to the wide choice and regular updates, the Internet makes it possible to make discreet, low-cost encounters at any time and in any place, as it offers "comfortable and secure anonymity[7]". What's more, the Internet obviously makes police action more laborious: "Prostitutes operating on the Net don't risk much, because even if they can be worried about soliciting, they're not a priority for the police[8]." Against this backdrop, many ex-street prostitutes and other "anonymous" prostitutes - including students - take up this activity on their own.

On the Net, the most visible offers of paid sex are those of "escorts". Originally, "escorting" consisted of "escorting" a client, i.e. accompanying a person (usually a man) to parties, restaurants, theaters, etc. In this context, the sexual relationship is not part of the contract, but remains an implicit intention, considered a private act between the escort and her client. This ambiguity justifies the fact that the escort is often likened to a "luxury prostitute", as she responds to a specific demand. "She is expected to be charming, beautiful and distinguished, but also to have intellectual qualities that enable her to accompany her clients, who are often socially well-off men[9]". Today, the "escort" business still exists, mainly through agencies. But the term "escort" is now used by all

---

7. Pascal Lardellier, *Le Cœur Net - Célibat et amour sur le Web*, Paris, Belin, 2004, p. 65.

8. Extract from the "notes d'intention" by author and director Yann Reuzeau for his play *Les Débutantes - Prostituées en quelques clics*, performed from November 2006 to February 2007 at the Manufacture des Abbesses in Paris.

9. Christelle Schaff, *Prostitution en France : l'enquête*, Éditions de la Lagune, 2007, p. 50.

prostitutes operating on the Net, whatever the "level" of their service. As a result, the term "escort" hides a wide range of realities: "Former street prostitutes driven off the street, professionals with busy schedules, foreigners exploited by networks[10], or occasional 'night beauties'[11]."

Escorts, whether "professional" or "amateur" like Laura, solicit and communicate through advertisements on specialized or general sites that include a section called "venal encounters" or "adult encounters". These ads mainly contain specific information about the services on offer. For example, we find the measurements of the escort, her age, the region or town in which she works, her availability, her rates, and sometimes a brief paragraph detailing her services and her "taboos[12]".

---

10. Of course, not all Internet prostitutes are independent: many work on behalf of "agencies", and some are under pressure from pimps, particularly with the establishment of "tours", veritable slave networks. On-tour" prostitute: A prostitute/escort who works for a pimp. The pimp installs her for a period - more or less short - in a hotel in a major Western city, where she receives a large number of clients on a daily basis (often more than 10 per day), then moves her to another city. Recruitment networks (mainly in Eastern Europe) and solicitation are carried out via the Web. The words "on tour" indicate that the prostitute is "on tour", making the "rounds" of major Western cities. In May 2000, a complementary office to the OCRETH (Office Central de Répression de la Traite des Êtres Humains) was set up to combat crime linked to new technologies. The OCLCTIC (Office Central de Lutte contre la Criminalité liée aux Techno-logies de l'Information et de la Communication) is responsible for dealing with petty crime and pimping.
11. Matthieu Franchon and Andreas Bitesnich, "Salariées le jour, escort girls la nuit", *Choc* (weekly), June 28 2007, no. 87, pp. 26-33.
12. In escorting jargon, "taboos" refer to sexual practices that the escort refuses to engage in as part of a venal relationship. In contrast, the term "taboo-free" refers to an escort who accepts all kinds of practices.

A number of escorts also have their own website or blog[13].
These personalized sites, generally basic in design and
interface, often present themselves in the same way. First, a
window opens, stating that the user must be of legal age to
proceed. Upon entering the site, a text, often written by the
escort herself, gives a more or less detailed presentation of
herself. Some simply describe themselves physically, while
others describe their interests, their marital status, their
reasons for prostituting themselves... This text also enables
the escort to set out her expectations with regard to the venal
encounter and the customer's behavior (meeting conditions,
tastes in sexual practices, type of man...). Next, a number
of headings specify the nature of the service offered by the
escort. Generally speaking, we find a list of possible services
and those that the escort refuses to perform; rates (by the
hour, evening, night or more); availability ("working hours");
and finally the contact page where the escort enters her e-mail
and/or cell phone number. The "photo gallery" often illus-
trates the blog and shows the escort in different lights. We can
see that very few "non-professional" escorts show their faces
in their photographs. Generally speaking, those who choose
to hide their faces do so mainly to preserve their identity,
because those around them are not aware of their prostitution and/or escorting is not their only activity. Often, these

---

13. *Blog* : A *website* made up of a collection of posts arranged in chronological
order. Each post (also called a "note" or "article") is an addition to the blog, like
a diary or journal. The *blogger* (i.e., the person who keeps the blog) writes a text,
often enriched with *hyperlinks* and multimedia elements, which readers can generally comment on.

Student Prostitution in the Age of the Internet

women have another "official" activity (student, for example) and prostitute themselves on an occasional basis (a few paid appointments per month).

For these "occasional prostitutes" - secretaries, housewives, lawyers, job-seekers, students, etc. - prostitution remains a secondary activity. From this perspective, the occasional woman is generally independent (she works for herself, on her own account) and prostitution is a personal choice, more or less conditioned, but a rational choice nonetheless. In this regard, Malika Nor[14] points out that occasional independent prostitutes are generally unknown to social services (which is why no organization, institutional or associative, has a precise idea of what student prostitution really is). The author adds that this kind of "voluntary prostitution is generally motivated by money, either because this activity proves to be extremely luxurious and lucrative, or because for these people it only represents a source of income that is complementary or necessary to a subsistence minimum".

The choice of prostitution - the possibility of leading a "double life" - is undoubtedly facilitated by the Internet. According to Yann Reuzeau's analysis, "today, many prostitutes start out on the Internet. Many of them would never have done so without this "deceptively" virtual opportunity [...], because the great novelty of the Internet is that it opens up this profession to absolutely anyone. A basic computer, an Internet connection, two or three photos,

---

14. Malika Nor, *La Prostitution*, Paris, ed. Le Cavalier Bleu, 2001, p. 54.

My Great Education

a solid 15 minutes, and voilà, you're an escort[15]!" In fact, according to Laura's testimony, it was while surfing the Web that she quickly and easily came across a multitude of explicit advertisements. Driven by the need for money and curiosity, while feeling "protected" behind her computer screen, Laura found on the Internet *the solution [she] was waiting for*: "*comfort, and fast…*".

At first glance, it may seem surprising to find students in the prostitution arena. However, we know that this population is far from "rolling in money", and many of them have a "job" in addition to their university obligations[16]. What's more, most of the jobs on offer that are compatible with a student's schedule are not very lucrative, or even underpaid. Consequently, it's not so surprising to think that "for a young person in a fragile economic situation, the temptation is great when you see the attraction of the sums involved in this type of activity[17]".

---

15. This voluntary, amateur prostitution is the subject of her latest play. It features Marion, a 19-year-old medical student who, in order to pursue her studies, occasionally prostitutes herself via the Internet. Yann Reuzeau, *Les Débutantes - Prostituées en quelques clics*, play (2006), performed from November 2006 to February 2007 at La Manufac-ture des Abbesses, Paris.
16. According to the Observatoire de la Vie Étudiante (OVE): In France, 47% of students have a salaried job alongside their studies, and 15% of them work at least six months a year, at least part-time.
17. Christelle Schaff, *op. cit.* p. 140.

2. Who are the students who prostitute themselves on the Internet?

It's difficult to establish a "typical profile" of the student prostitute on the Net. However, one thing is clear: almost all online ads are placed by young women. Moreover, if we look at the press articles published on the subject over the course of the year, the authors make no reference whatsoever to male student prostitution. For many, the practice of prostitution is only "a women's issue", and, by extension, student prostitution only concerns female students. Admittedly, ads for student prostitutes are virtually invisible on the Web, but that doesn't mean that male student prostitution doesn't exist[18] . In this respect, rather than thinking of prostitution as "reserved" only for women, we need to question the reality of this difference between the sexes. If women are over-represented on the supply side of prostitution, and men over-represented on the demand side, it's because prostitution is rooted in a complex system of unequal gender relations. In this system, female sexuality - socially constructed - remains under the control of men's "drives" - claiming to be "natural" when in

---

18. For my study, I met a young student who had been a street prostitute for two years and who now uses the Internet - deemed "less risky than the street" - to find clients. He doesn't have an ad or a blog, but logs on to "gay" dating sites to make new contacts. In his view, the under-representation of men - and therefore students - as "providers" of "paid sexual services" is a story of supply and demand. *"Male demand for 'free' heterosexual sex is greater than supply* - hence the institution of female prostitution to 'fill' this gap. *On the other hand, the gap between demand and supply of "free" male homosexual sex is smaller. As a result, there are fewer male prostitutes than there are female prostitutes, as the demand for "free sex" competes with the supply of "free sex".*

fact they are socially constructed. Awareness of these mechanisms of domination and power of the male class over the female class is essential to understanding prostitution and the issue of student prostitution.

Having said this, we know that the majority of student prostitutes are female. What's more, according to the various journalistic sources gathered on this subject, female students who prostitute themselves do so essentially out of a need for money, and because they lack the time to hold a sufficiently profitable job alongside their studies. To explain students' choice of prostitution, the media emphasize their economic precariousness, linked to the ever-increasing cost of living. These are the reasons why Laura decides to prostitute herself. Like many students at the public university, Laura comes from a middle-class background, and her standard of living depends heavily on that of her family. According to institutional criteria and definitions, however, her family is not "needy", since both parents have full-time jobs and earn incomes deemed "sufficient" to support all family members. In today's reality, however, even on two minimum incomes, many of these "average" families have to learn to "tighten their belts" to live decently.

However, economic insecurity - linked to the student's social background[19] - is not the only reason why students choose to prostitute. Indeed, not all "financially challenged" students prostitute themselves! And not all student escorts have a vital

---

19. Assistance from parents and other family members accounts for nearly 44.6% of students' resources [CREDOC figure, 1992] - Olivier Galland and Marco Oberti, *Les Étudiants*, Paris, La Découverte, 1996, p. 67.

need for money[20]. In this context, the image of the "poor student" portrayed in the media needs to be nuanced.

3. WHY DO FEMALE STUDENTS CHOOSE PROSTITUTION?

According to my study, student prostitution is a response to various ruptures, more or less significant, in their life history. Thus, the reasons and motivations that led them to make this choice can vary from one experience to another, contributing to the diversity of student prostitutes' profiles.

For some, like Laura, prostitution is above all a "utilitarian" goal - earning money to continue their studies. For some, it represents a kind of "forbidden fantasy", enabling them to break with traditional family values. For others, it's "revenge" on the men with whom they've had gratuitous relationships. Through these various realities (which are not exhaustive), we can identify three patterns of rupture: social and financial ruptures, ruptures in relation to family morality, and ruptures in relation to gratuitous love relationships. Obviously, these patterns are not fixed, and some students combine two or three of these ruptures.

a) Social and financial disruption - Students willing to do anything to succeed

To finance their studies, pay the rent or make ends meet, some students are turning to prostitution. One of the causes

---

20. For my study, I met two student escorts whose primary goal in prostitution is not financial gain. Both are (easily) financially supported by their parents.

of this practice is certainly linked to the impoverishment of the student population. Guillaume Houzel - Chairman of the Observatoire de la Vie Étudiante (OVE) - comments: "For some years now, we've been seeing increasing pressure on students' purchasing power. With the rise in property prices, their housing expenses are increasing... but not the amount of their grants[21]." According to the Dauriac report[22] on the economic insecurity of students, 100,000 students in higher education live below the poverty line, which is set at around 650 euros per month per person. According to the OVE, more than 45,000 students are currently living in extreme poverty, and 225,000 are struggling to finance their studies[23]. It should be remembered that this impoverishment affects a certain category of students, namely those whose parents are unwilling or unable to support them financially, and who consequently have to fend for themselves - or nearly so - to meet their needs and pursue their studies.

Like Laura, student escorts from working- and middle-class backgrounds experience a number of social and financial shortcomings in their current lives as students, which compromise - to a greater or lesser extent - their pursuit of

---

21. Jean-Marc Philibert, "La prostitution gagne les bancs de la fac", *Le Figaro*, October 30, 2006, p. 11.

22. Jean-François Dauriac was successively director of the Crous for the Créteil academy (from 1992 to 2001) and then for the Versailles academy (until 2004). In 2000, Claude Allègre - then Minister of Education - commissioned J.-F. Dauriac to draw up a report on the economic situation of students in France, with a view to implementing a "Student Social Plan". Jean-François Dauriac, *Note de synthèse du rapport au ministre de l'Éducation nationale, de la Recherche et de la Technologie sur la mise en œuvre du plan social étudiant*, Paris, 2000.

23. Jean-Marc Philibert, *op. cit.* - France currently has 2,200,000 students.

Student Prostitution in the Age of the Internet

higher education. For these students, academic success is of paramount importance. In addition to personal gratification, pursuing higher education offers them the opportunity to establish their ambition - to "make something of themselves" - and to secure a more "comfortable" lifestyle than the one they experienced in their families. However, neither these students nor their families have the financial resources to fully realize this ambition. In this context, prostitution proves to be an alternative to "*pursue [their] dreams*".

Many authors[24] agree that students are not equal when it comes to financing their studies, and that the advantages - particularly economic - enjoyed by young people from wealthy backgrounds, but lacking by those from less privileged backgrounds, result in unequal access to higher education. The French government, aware of this "inequality of opportunity", has set up a system to provide financial assistance to certain young people (scholarships based on social criteria, merit-based scholarships, housing allowances, etc.), thus offering them a "fundamental tool for the social elevator[25]". However, this system is obviously

---

24. Examples include Pierre Bourdieu and Jean-Claude Passeron, *Les Héritiers : les étudiants de la culture*, Paris, Éditions de Minuit, 1989; Raymond Boudon, *L'Inégalité des chances - La mobilité sociale dans les sociétés industrielles*, Paris, Armand Colin, 1979; François Dubet, "Les étudiants", *in* F. Dubet *et al*, *Universités et villes*, Paris, L'Harmattan, 1994; Stéphane Beaud, *80 % au bac... et après?*, Paris, La Découverte, 2003; M. Euriat and C. Thelot, "Le recrutement social de l'élite scolaire en France", *Revue française de sociologie*, XXXVI-3, July-September 1995, pp. 403-438.

25. In 2006, student aid amounted to 6 billion euros, benefiting 2.2 million students. Source: Laurent Wauquiez, *Les aides aux étudiants : comment relancer l'ascenseur social*, Paris, 2006.

not without flaws (remember that Laura is not entitled to scholarships) and only partially covers students' needs. Over five years, compulsory expenses - registration fees, social security, accommodation, meals at university restaurants, etc. - have increased by 23%, while university grants and housing allowances have risen by only 10%. Given this state of affairs, it is imperative for many students to have a paid job in addition to their studies.

In 2003, 45.5% of French students were gainfully employed during the academic year (excluding the summer vacations[26]). Through Laura's testimony, who works fifteen hours a week in a telemarketing company in addition to her twenty hours of university classes and the time she spends studying, we can see just how much having a "student job" handicaps her from completing her studies properly. She is perpetually tired and plays with her health. This reality echoes the work carried out by the Observatoire de la Vie Étudiante (Student Life Observatory), which points out that holding a paid job while studying increases "the risk of failure or dropping out[27]". These risks result from the competition - particularly in terms of time - between the "student job" and the demands of university work. According to the OVE, this is the context in which the notion of student precariousness should be understood. From this point of view, prostitution enables students from more modest social backgrounds to

---

26. Claude Grignon (Chairman of the Scientific Committee of the OVE), *Les étudiants en difficulté : Pauvreté et précarité* - Rapport au ministre de la Jeunesse, de l'Éducation nationale et de la Recherche, Paris, 2003.
27. Claude Grignon, *op. cit.*

pursue their studies under favorable material conditions - daily needs such as rent and food are covered - while leaving them enough time to work on their courses and hope to pass their university year.

While the strategy may seem logical, it does raise questions about the price these middle- and working-class students have to pay to access higher education and graduate. Clearly, the social elevator and the paths to "success" are far from equal for all!

b) Breaking away from family morality - Students eager to break away from the shackles of the past

For some students, prostitution is not directly linked to a need for money, but rather to a desire to break with traditional family values and satisfy a "forbidden fantasy".

Today, even if sexuality is not "free", since - like all social interaction - it is embedded in a certain number of relationships (gender, class, generation, cultural...), it is perceived as being, *a priori,* less and less codified[28]. In this regard, Michel Bozon points out that one of the major changes in generational relations between the 1960s and the 2000s is that "the parents' generation has given up setting restrictive standards for young people[29]". The possibility of

---

28. Thomas Laqueur, *La Fabrique du sexe - Essai sur le corps et le genre en Occident,* Paris, Gallimard, 1992.

29. Parents do, however, keep a watchful eye on their children's sexual practices, particularly with regard to the risks of sexually transmitted infections or unplanned pregnancy. - Michel Bozon, *Sociologie de la sexualité,* Paris, Armand Colin, 2005, p. 54.

experiencing "real youth" has gradually become widespread, and the "private autonomy" of these young people is generally accepted. In this context, parents no longer condemn their children's active love lives - which can sometimes even take place under their own roof. Of course, this does not apply to all contemporary families. Some retain traditional values - linked to religious morality - and show a more exacerbated control over their children's sexuality.

In these conservative families, young people's entry into sexuality takes place under the watchful eye and control of relatives (and possibly elders). Parents set the rules by which their children - especially girls - can access this statutory activity of maturity[30] . In this context, children's dating and outings - especially in adolescence - are often tightly controlled by parents. Similarly, the subject of sexuality remains taboo and is rarely brought to the fore in family discussions.

For students from this type of family, prostitution is seen as a means of emancipating themselves from family values and norms. By prostituting themselves, these students set themselves apart from the parental model, thus affirming their desire for autonomy in relation to their own. From this perspective, they want to take charge of their own lives - their intimate lives at any rate - and participate in the construction of their personal identity.

---

30. Michel Bozon, *op. cit.*

c) A break with love and male/female relationships - Disillusioned and disillusioned female students

For some student escorts, prostitution is a way of filling an emotional and sexual void. Often, these young women have been disappointed by their previous love affairs and "gratuitous relationships", in which they feel they were not appreciated for their true worth. In effect, they "offered themselves freely" to men who failed to meet their expectations of commitment and mutual recognition. In such relationships, they felt "betrayed", "abused", because respect and consideration for themselves were absent.

Nevertheless, these students want to remain sexually active, and improve their sexuality by learning new practices and experiences. In this context, their practice of prostitution makes sense. Money in sexual relations clarifies the situation. These student escorts know that their prostitution encounters do not go beyond the terms of the "contract", and that it is pointless to hope for "a story" beyond the venal rendezvous. So they can live the encounter intensely, focusing on their own sexual pleasure and not worrying about what comes after.

4. What's in it for us?

Whatever the reasons and motivations that lead students to prostitute themselves, this practice cannot be considered a harmless act. Laura's misadventures illustrate this point. Likewise, while the choice is a personal one, it is - like all choices - part of a particular context. Prostitution doesn't happen by chance. The need for money, the desire to get away from it all, or disappointment in love relationships, are not enough on their own to explain why some students turn to prostitution.

According to a study on "the risk of prostitution among young people[31]", there is a "basic terrain" in which a certain number of dysfunctions - linked to the personal and social history of individuals - "germinate", leading some young people into prostitution. The survey shows that these "dysfunctions" are varied and self-influencing. They can include "biographical accidents" (physical, moral and sexual violence), problems of identity and identification with parental models, social isolation, psychological fragility, social disqualification by the family to which they belong, distorted social representations of modes of success, or the fact of having - in one's network - acquaintances belonging to the world of prostitution.

The choice of prostitution is therefore not the result of a single element, but rather a combination of various personal and social ruptures, of varying degrees of severity. Paradoxically, for some, prostitution becomes an alternative that gives meaning to their practices and life choices. Students' involvement in prostitution takes place in a particular context, at a particular time in their lives. While this activity enables them to get out of a "difficult" situation, it is not without consequences. To date, no studies have been carried out to

---

31. This study, carried out by a French association, does not refer to students, but targets young people aged 18 to 25 who are being monitored by social services and are in a precarious economic and social situation. ANRS - Service Insertion Jeunes - Association Nationale de Réadaptation Sociale, *Le risque prostitutionnel chez les jeunes de 18-25 ans* (étude exploratoire), Paris, 1995.

track the progress of these people, or to ascertain the consequences - both individual and social - that these practices may have in the long term.

5. ANY SOLUTIONS?

Recourse to prostitution - whatever its form - reveals a certain social malaise. We have seen that this practice is at the heart of social relations where male and economic domination reign supreme. Faced with this state of affairs, we can only hope for a change in mentality to curb the inequalities at play. We know that education is one of the keys to changing mentalities. However, the means deployed by public authorities to bring about a change in attitudes in these areas remain insufficient (or even non-existent).

In our society, the subject of sexuality is still largely taboo, and remains imbued with sexist beliefs and stereotypes that imprison both women and men in differentiated, hierarchical gender roles. Modesty, the possibility of sexual continence, moderation and the absence of desire are still considered to be "natural" qualities for women. Conversely, desire, aggressiveness and activity are defined as the hallmarks of the male individual[32]. If more institutions - and more individuals - were to take account of the gender dimension in their analyses and actions, sexuality could be viewed in an egalitarian and libertarian light.

---

32. Michel Bozon, *op. cit.* p. 25.

For almost ten years, the various governments in power have been seeking to "transform" universities, citing as their official reason the need to combat the economic insecurity of young people. However, the various reforms proposed (the LMD reform, the law on "equal opportunities" and its famous Contrat Première Embauche, and today's law on university autonomy, etc.) only serve to reinforce the existing divide between students from working-class backgrounds and those from privileged backgrounds. If the government's plan were truly egalitarian for all students, a number of concrete measures would be put in place: the system of aid based on social criteria would be upgraded (students like Laura would then be eligible for grants), the number of places in cité-U would be significantly increased, "student jobs" would be properly remunerated and better adapted to the needs and skills of each individual, and so on.

But when it comes to issues of gender equality and wealth equality, leaders are still cautious…

Table of contents

Best sellers Max Milo Editions

Hitler's banker, Jean-François Bouchard

Confessions of a forger, Éric Piedoie Le Tiec

The Koran and the flesh, Ludovic-Mohamed Zahed

Governing by fake news, Jacques Baud

Governing by chaos, Collectif

A political history of food, Paul Ariès

Mad in U.S.A.: The ravages of the "American model",
Michel Desmurget

Mondial soccer club geopolitics, Kévin Veyssière

Putin: Game master?, Jacques Braud

Treatise on the three impostors: Moses, Jesus, Muhammad,
The Spirit of Spinoza

TV Lobotomy, Michel Desmurget